THE END OF THE WORLD
—*from the beginning*—

JOHN MARINELLI

The End of the World from the Beginning
Copyright © 2021 John Marinelli
Ocala, Florida
All rights reserved.
First Edition: 2022

Print ISBN: 978-1-0879-8598-5
eBook ISBN: 978-1-0880-0155-4

Cover and Formatting: Streetlight Graphics

This book is protected under US copyright laws. Any reproduction or other use is prohibited without the written permission of the author.

No part of this book may be reproduced, scanned, or distributed in any printed or electronic form without permission. Please do not participate in or encourage piracy of copyrighted materials in violation of the author's rights. Thank you for respecting the hard work of this author.

More books and Christian Ministry at
www.marinellichristianbooks.com

PREFACE

The purpose of this book is to call attention to the "End of The World" and what the Bible has to say about those events that lead up to the end. The author will discuss such topics as The Anti-Christ, The Battle of the Ages, The Devil's ToolBox, The Origin of Evil, Overcoming Your Adversary, The 2nd Coming of Christ and much more.

The goal of this book is to inform the reader of future events and to educate new believers as to preparation for the coming of the end of days.

The author's hope is that every reader will grow in grace, become, "Born Again" and strengthened by the Biblical truth presented.

TABLE OF CONTENTS

Introduction	vii
Chapter One: The Origin of Evil	1
Chapter Two: The Beast Within	13
Chapter Three: The Devils Toolbox	23
Chapter Four: Dead Men Walking	47
Chapter Five: Portrait Of The Damned	55
Chapter Six: The Anti-Christ	69
Chapter Seven: Battle Of The Ages	82
Chapter Eight: Life At The End of The Age	115
Chapter Nine: Overcoming The Enemy Of Your Soul	128
Chapter Ten: Divine Appointments	132
Chapter Eleven: Finding God's Will For Your Life	141
Chapter Twelve: The Rapture of The Church	163
Conclusion	185
Gallery of Anointed Christian Poems	199
About The Author	211

INTRODUCTION

People have been talking about the "End of The World" since time began. Some folks I know say this final event in man's history will never happen. They say that we will have a world without end where folks will rise up to a better self and eventually be as gods.

Others say that the end of days is when you die. It is then that a person ceases to exist. They have no more knowledge of life or the future. Soul sleep is part of this thought ideology.

However, most of the normal thinking folks, like me and hopefully you, believe that there will come a day when the heavens will pass away and the earth will burn with fervent heat and life on earth will no longer exist. This train of thought is based upon Biblical truth that began thousands of years ago, even before Jesus prophesied concerning the end. One of my wife's friends, when she heard about my book said, "It sounds like Global Warming to me." <u>Now that's funny</u>!

Predictions of the end of time or the end of the world have been going on since the 1st millennium. All through the centuries, Pastors, Popes, Priest, Prophets and regular folk have set a date for the end of days. Guess what? They were all wrong. Trying to foretell this future event is impossible. Why? Because Jesus said, in answer to his disciples question about the end of the world, *"But of that day and hour knoweth no man, no, not the angels of heaven, but my Father only.* Matthew 24:36

Many of the predictions were made as a causal effect from some natural disaster, the Y2K dilemma at the turn of the century, Meteors from space, Man made wars, and several other events.

The end of the world predictions on record exceeds 200 and even come from some modern day notable personalities such as Jerry Falwell, Billy Graham, John Hagee, Pat Robertson and several Catholic Popes. Mixed in the list are several non-Christian groups and lots of regular folk that never made national or worldwide recognition.

We all want to know when this event will happen but no one on earth has the answer. Imagine if we did. We could set our hearts to get right with God and prepare for what is to come. Sadly, many will cry out, "Let's eat, drink and be merry for tomorrow we die." They will still reject God's love and grace and even shake their fist at the creator of all things.

The end of the world is commonly known as, "The Day of The Lord." Here's what the Bible says about that.

1. "For yourselves know perfectly that *the day of the Lord* so cometh as a *thief in the night*.... For when they shall say, Peace and safety; then sudden destruction will come. I Thessalonians 5:2
2. "But the day of the Lord will come as a *thief in the night*; in the which the heavens shall pass away with a great noise, and the elements shall melt with fervent heat" 2 Peter 3:10.
3. Matthew 24 also speaks of that day and says it will come as a thief in the night. The assumption is that it will be at a time when most folks are not paying attention.

The times leading up to, "That Day" and the reasons why, "That Day" has to come will be discussed in the following 12 chapters.

Here's what the apostle Paul said… "For when they shall say, Peace and safety; then sudden destruction cometh upon them, as travail upon a woman with child; and they shall not escape. But ye, brethren, are not in darkness, that that day should overtake you as a thief. " I Thessalonians 5:3-4

As believers in Christ and followers of his teachings, we are not supposed to be ignorant of future events. We are not supposed to be in darkness or be overtaken by the coming of the Lord. We are supposed to be watching and praying and looking for the signs that precede this event.

The Signs of His Coming

1. And ye shall hear of **wars and rumors of wars**: see that ye be not troubled: for all these things must come to pass, but the end is not yet.." *Matthew 24:6* (You should read the full chapter.)

2. "Let no man deceive you by any means: for that day shall not come, except **there come a falling away first**, and that man of sin be revealed, the son of perdition; Who opposeth and exalteth himself above all that is called God, or that is worshipped; so that he as God sitteth in the temple of God, shewing himself that he is God." *2 Thess. 2:3-4 (*I believe that this is a falling away from true faith in God.)

3. "And **there shall be signs** in the sun, and in the moon, and in the stars; and upon the earth **distress of nations**, with perplexity; the sea and the waves roaring;" *Luke 21:25-26*

4. "But the day of the Lord will come as a thief in the night; in the which **the heavens shall pass away** with a great noise, **he earth also and the works that are therein shall be burned up.**" and the elements shall melt with fervent heat, *2 Peter 3:10*

5. "**For many shall come in my name**, saying, I am Christ; and shall deceive many." *Matthew 24:5* (I believe these folks are

professing Christian in title only. They do not believe in their hearts nor do they walk by faith.)

6. "For **nation shall rise against nation**, and kingdom against kingdom: and **there shall be famines, and pestilences, and earthquakes**, in divers places." *Matthew 24:7*

7. "And then shall **many be offended, and shall betray one another**, and shall hate one another." *Matthew 24:10*

8. "And this **gospel of the kingdom shall be preached in all the world** for a witness unto all nations; and then shall the end come." *Matthew 24:14*

9. "For **there shall arise false Christs, and false prophets**, and shall shew great signs and wonders; insomuch that, if it were possible, they shall deceive the very elect." *Matthew 24:24* (The world is full of false religions and teachers)

10. "For then shall be **great tribulation**, such as was not since the beginning of the world to this time, no, nor ever shall be." *Matthew 24:21*

Not to worry. Jesus is coming again to gather his followers in a glorious event called "The Rapture." We will be spared from the wrath of God that will fall on the ungodly. See chapter 12 for more details.

Question? Why do folks do bad things? Who says what we do is bad or good? Is life made up of just good and evil? Where does good come from? Where does evil come from?

It's my belief that you cannot really understand why the world will end until you know how and why it was created. Looking at the beginning is the 1st step in understanding the end.

Life is filled with questions and some of us never find the answerers until it's too late. We seem to be in a never-ending valley of decisions faced with making choices without sufficient knowledge.

I guess that's why there are so many different opinions on so many different subjects.

I think it is important to ask some questions. Here are a few to ponder:

1. Will the world really end?
2. Why will the earth be destroyed?
3. Who or what will kill every living thing?
4. When will this destruction happen?
5. Will the end come in my lifetime?
6. Why can't life go on as it has for centuries?
7. What has the human race done to deserve total destruction?

Let's begin with how evil fits into the end of the world scenario.

We all have a free will to choose and are held accountable for those choices. No one ever said, as a child, "I want to grow up to be a drunk or drug addict or prostitute or child molester or mass murder." The choices they made led them down that road until they became what they were thinking. "As a man thinks in his heart, so is he". Proverbs 23:7

Chapter One is a discussion of the Origin, Nature and Destiny of Evil. We will look at where evil came from, why it exists, and its mission. This is important because evil is the reason why the world will be destroyed. It is the motivator for God's wrath.

I will be using the Bible as my source of inspiration and documentation. I will also offer some personal opinions and suggestions. Together, we will discover how to identify evil and resist it so it does not lead us down a path of destruction. To do otherwise is to miss the truths of God relative to the end of all things.

CHAPTER ONE

THE ORIGIN OF EVIL

Definition of Evil

Synonyms Include:

According to the dictionary, evil is defined as profoundly immoral.

> wicked, bad, wrong, immoral, sinful, foul, vile, dishonorable, corrupt, iniquitous, depraved, reprobate, villainous, nefarious, vicious, malicious; and lots more
>
> Being Moral is to demonstrate a high ethical standard of conduct. This standard can only be measured by the character of God. Thus, immorality is that which defiles the righteous standard established by God.

AS WE LOOK FOR THE origin of evil, we must realize that it is a matter of morality. We must be able to distinguish between man's morality and God's morality. God's morality is called Righteousness. Man's morality misses this mark or standard. It can shift and even change with the moods of society. One day it is immoral to have and abortion and the next it is consider ok or normal.

We must align ourselves to the morality of God. Why? Because he never changes. He, unlike man, does not waver in character or personality. He is always good, always righteous, always truthful, always right. A good picture is to contrast light with darkness. God is light and there is no darkness in him. He is pure in every way.

Now, lets look at evil. It is anti-God. It does not accept God as the standard for good or should I say righteousness? It projects itself as a replacement for God. It will deceive men and women into thinking that it is good when it is far from being good.

So, what is evil?…It is the rejection of God and all that he stands for. This attitude is called "SIN" and it is first of all aimed at God; to dishonor him and steal his throne and take control over all things including mankind.

Where did evil begin? According to the Bible, it all began in the heart of Lucifer; an archangel of God that some scholars believe led the worship in heaven. He was magnificent in every way. He led 1/3 of all the angels in a rebellion against God that ended up with all that rebelled being cast out of the heavenly realm. This all happened because Lucifer wanted to be God. Thus he rebelled and tried to take over as God. This was considered the very first sin and it met with swift judgment.

Here are a few supporting scriptures that reveal the truth.

1. And he, (Jesus), said unto them, (His disciples),"I beheld Satan, as lightning, fall from heaven." Luke 10:18

2. "And there was war in heaven: Michael and his angels fought against the dragon; and the dragon fought and his angels, and prevailed not; neither was their place found any more in heaven. And the great dragon was cast out, that old serpent, called the Devil, and Satan, which deceives the whole world: he was cast out into the earth, and his angels were cast out with him." Revelation 12:7-9

3. "How art thou fallen from heaven, O Lucifer, son of the morning! How art thou cut down to the ground, which didst weaken the nations! For thou hast said in thine heart, I will ascend into heaven, I will exalt my throne above the stars of God: I will sit also upon the mount of the congregation, in the sides of the north: I will ascend above the heights of the clouds; I will be like the most

High. Yet thou shalt be brought down to hell, to the sides of the pit." Isaiah 14:12-15

4. "And the angels which kept not their first estate, but left their own habitation, he hath reserved in everlasting chains under darkness unto the judgment of the great day." Jude v-6

5. "By the multitude of thy merchandise they have filled the midst of thee with violence, and thou hast sinned: therefore I will cast thee as profane out of the mountain of God: and I will destroy thee, O covering cherub, from the midst of the stones of fire. Thine heart was lifted up because of thy beauty, thou hast corrupted thy wisdom by reason of thy brightness: I will cast thee to the ground, I will lay thee before kings, that they may behold thee." Ezekiel 28:16-17

By now you probably have noticed different names for evil. They are all the same entity. Evil started in one individual personality, a spiritual being. He sinned against God by trying to be God. Over the centuries that entity has taken on many different names.

There are a lot of folks that do not believe in the existence of a being that is evil. They think that evil comes from the hearts of men and women, boys and girls but not a supernatural being. Jesus spoke at length about this evil being. In fact, the Bible has many different names for him including:

- Lucifer, meaning "Morning Star" (Isaiah 14:12)
- Ruler of The Demons (Matthew 12:24)
- god of This World (2 Corinthians 4:4)
- Devil/Accuser (Matthew 4:1)
- Prince of the Power of the Air (Ephesians 2:2)
- Roaring Lion (1 Peter 5:8)
- The Serpent (Genesis 3:1)
- Dragon (Revelation 12:9; 20:2)

- Adversary (Job 1)
- The Tempter (Matthew 4:3)
- The anointed Cherub (Ezekiel 28:14)
- Beelzebub (Matthew 12:24)
- Belial (2 Corinthians 6:15)
- Wicked One (Matthew 13:19)
- Thief (John 10:10)

Lord of the Flies, the Anti-Christ and Father of Lies are also used to describe this evil being. Jesus referred to him as a thief and said "The thief comes only to steal and kill and destroy; I have come that they may have life, and have it to the full." John 10:10

Peter called him our adversary, the devil. "Be sober, be vigilant; because your adversary the devil, as a roaring lion, walks about, seeking whom he may devour: Whom resist stedfast in the faith, knowing that the same afflictions are accomplished in your brethren that are in the world." I Peter 5:8-9

A more detailed description of the many names attributed to the devil can be found in chapter seven.

This evil, being called the devil, first showed up in the Bible in the book of Genesis as the serpent who convinced Eve—who then convinced Adam—to eat forbidden fruit from the "tree of the knowledge." This all happened in the Garden of Eden. As the story goes, after Adam and Eve fell for the devil's conniving ways, they were banished from the Garden of Eden and doomed to a life of *mortality*.

The devil makes more appearances in the Bible, especially in the New Testament. Jesus and many of his apostles warned people to stay alert for the devil's cunning enticements. It was the devil who tempted Jesus in the wilderness to "fall down and worship him" in exchange for riches and glory. Jesus didn't fall for his deceptive suggestions.

Perhaps the most lasting images of the devil are associated with Hell, which the Bible refers to as a place of everlasting fire prepared for the devil and his angels. Still, the Bible doesn't state the devil will reign over hell, just that he'll eventually be banished there where he will suffer for all of eternity.

Throughout history, the devil's reputation as an evildoer hasn't changed much. Most Christians still believe he is responsible for much of the world's corruption and chaos.

What's important to realize is that this evil being is a defeated foe. That is evident from what the scriptures say…

Jesus Christ came for two purposes, "to seek and to save that which was lost" (Luke 19:10) and "that he might destroy the works of the devil" (1st John 3:8) "And having spoiled principalities and powers, he made a shew of them openly, triumphing over them in it." (Colossians 2:15)

This is why Peter says we can stand up to that "Roaring Lion", resist him and he will flee from us…because he has no power over us except what we give him. I Peter 5:8

Evil and Mankind

So, how did man become evil? Wasn't he created in the image of God who is Holy? It all started when Adam and Eve rebelled against God. I do not believe that they were just deceived by the devil and made a mistake. It may have started with deception but in the final analysis, they disobeyed God. ***Listen and learn.***

"And the Lord God took the man, and put him into the Garden of Eden to dress it and to keep it. And the Lord God commanded the man, saying, Of every tree of the garden thou may freely eat: But of the tree of the knowledge of good and evil, thou shalt not eat of it: for in the day that thou eat thereof thou shalt surely die." Genesis 2:16-17

As the story goes, they listened to the serpent (devil) who said they would be like God, knowing good and evil when they took the forbidden fruit. The irony of it all is that they were already like God, being made in his every image.

God never wanted man to know evil because it was immoral, unholy and against all that God is. If they experienced evil, they would no longer be in the image of God. They would forfeit their innocence and their character would change from good to evil. There was no in-between or neutrality. Any such rebellion would end in a state of mortality, which would lead to death.

Now see it all happening in real time through the pages of the Bible.

"Wherefore, as by one man sin entered into the world, and death by sin; and so death passed upon all men, for that all have sinned: (For until the law sin was in the world: but sin is not imputed when there is no law.) Nevertheless death reigned from Adam to Moses, even over them that had not sinned after the similitude of Adam's transgression, who is the figure of him that was to come." Romans 5:12-14

Death passed upon all men for all have sinned. That is the result of Adam's transgression…He lost the image of God and we were prevented from ever having it. An entire race fell from the grace of God. Instead of being or possessing a character of righteousness we now possess a character that is evil. No longer are we naturally good but rather bent on being our own god and doing our own thing, which is anti-God because it subverts the very plan of God to create man in his own image and likeness.

The nature of evil now exists in humanity. That affects all of society as we, now being our own gods, fight with each other to be the one and only supreme god. That's why Jesus said, " verily, verily, I say unto thee, except a man be born again, he cannot see the kingdom of God." John 3:3

Here's a Biblical example of what Jesus is saying, "And the light shineth in darkness; and the darkness comprehended it not." John 1:5 Darkness just does not understand light. So it is with the natural man. He just does not comprehend the things of God.

The Face of Evil

We see the face of evil all around us. The nightly news reveals its character every day. The Bible also tells us about the character of evil as it dwells within the hearts of the human race. Listen to the apostle Paul as he writes to the church of the Galatians.

"This I say then, walk in the Spirit, and ye shall not fulfill the lust of the flesh. For The flesh lusts against the Spirit, and the Spirit against the flesh: and these are contrary the one to the other: so that ye cannot do the things that ye would. But if ye be led of the Spirit, ye are not under the law.

Now the works of the flesh are manifest, which are these; adultery, fornication, uncleanness, lasciviousness, Idolatry, witchcraft, hatred, variance, emulations, wrath, strife, seditions, heresies, envying, murders, drunkenness, rebelling, and such like: of the which I tell you before, as I have also told you in time past, that they which do such things shall not inherit the kingdom of God. (*This is the face of evil and it raises its awful head in many individuals these days.*)

But the fruit of the Spirit is love, joy, peace, longsuffering, gentleness, goodness, faith, meekness, temperance: against such there is no law. And they that are Christ's have crucified the flesh with the affections and lusts.

"If we live in the Spirit, let us also walk in the Spirit. Let us not be desirous of vain glory, provoking one another, envying one another." Gal.5:15-26

Paul contrasts the works of the flesh, which is the character of the fallen man, with the fruit of the Spirit, which is the character of God. Adam was created in the image and likeness of God. He possessed God's very nature, his character, which is Love, Joy, Peace, Longsuffering, Gentleness, Goodness, Faith, Meekness, and Temperance. This is what Adam lost when he disobeyed God. This is what we gain when we are, "Born Again"

The Mission of Evil

Believe it or not, evil is on a mission. Jesus taught us this when he said, "The thief cometh not, but for to steal, and to kill, and to destroy: I am come that they might have life, and that they might have it more abundantly. John 10:10

Jesus contrasted his mission with that of "the thief", which is another title for evil personified. The mission of evil is to Steal, Kill and Destroy. The devil wants to steal your peace, kill your joy and destroy your love so you become like him, evil and full of hate. However, Jesus came that we might have life and that the life we experience be in abundance. His destiny for us is to live not die; to laugh not cry; to love not hate; to be full of goodness not evil.

It's important to know that we were created as the temple of God. Man was to be the throne of God upon the earth. Our hearts were created with the capacity for God to dwell there in perfect harmony.

Satan's mission was to first block God from dwelling on his earthly throne, the hearts of men and second to seat himself on that same throne, man's heart thus ruling the earth and its inhabitance. His power now comes from fallen man whose nature is evil. (Like father/like son) They are both the same.

The Final Destiny of Evil

Evil will not persist forever. It has an end and that end is soon to come. Here's what the Bible says:

1. **Revelation 20:10** "And the devil that deceived them was cast into the lake of fire and brimstone, where the beast and the false prophet are, and shall be tormented day and night for ever and ever." Revelation 20:14-15 "Then Death and Hades were cast into the lake of fire. This is the second death.

2. **Matthew 25:41** "Then he will say to those on his left, 'Depart from me, you accursed, into the eternal fire that has been prepared for the devil and his angels!

3. **Revelation 20:10** And the devil who deceived them was thrown into the lake of fire and sulfur, where the beast and the false prophet are too, and they will be tormented there day and night forever and ever.

Good will always overcome evil because good is the nature of God and God never loses. At the end of the day, *God wins.*

We are in a life and death struggle with the forces evil. Our destiny depends upon how we fight and live our lives here on this earth. The forces of devil can take the unsaved at his or her will because they are children of darkness but the "Born Again" believer is washed in the blood of Christ and has the Holy Spirit of promise inside of him. He or she can overcome. Here are the support scriptures to prove what I am saying.

The Seal of Promise…"Who hath also sealed us, and given the earnest of the Spirit in our hearts." 11 Corinthians 1:22 "In him you also, when you heard the word of truth, the gospel of your salvation, and believed in him, were sealed with the promised Holy Spirit, who is the guarantee of our inheritance until we acquire possession of it, to the praise of his glory." Ephesians 1:13

The Holy Spirit is God's seal on his people, His claim on us as his very own. The Greek word translated "earnest" in these passages is *arrhabōn* which means "a pledge," that is, part of the purchase money or property given in advance as security for the rest. The gift of the Spirit to believers is a down payment on our heavenly inheritance, which Christ has promised us and secured for us at the cross. It is because the Spirit has sealed us that we are assured of our salvation. *No one can break the seal of God.*

The Greater Spirit... "Ye are of God, little children, and have overcome them: because greater is he that is in you, than he that is in the world." 1 John 4:4 "But ye are not in the flesh, but in the Spirit, if so be that the Spirit of God dwell in you. Now if any man has not the Spirit of Christ, he is none of his." Romans 8:9

The Holy Spirit is inside of us guiding us and leading us along the narrow path to glory. His counsel is greater than any evil spirit that attacks our souls from without. "However, when he, the Spirit of truth, is come, he will guide you into all truth: for he shall not speak of himself; but whatever he shall hear, that shall he speak: and he will show you things to come." John 16:13

The Overcomes... "And they, (The believers), overcame him, (The devil), by the blood of the Lamb, and by the word of their testimony; and they loved not their lives unto the death." Revelation 12:12

The Victory... "Be sober, be vigilant; because your adversary the devil, as a roaring lion, walks about, seeking whom he may devour. Resist him, *standing firm in the faith*, because you know that the family of believers throughout the world is undergoing the same kind of sufferings." I Peter 5:8-9

So, the origin of evil is Lucifer, that wicked angel that rebelled against God and led 1/3 of all the Heavenly Host in a battle against God that ended with all of them being cast out of Heaven.

The nature of evil is sin that manifest itself in wickedness, adultery, fornication, uncleanness, lasciviousness, Idolatry, witchcraft, hatred, variance, emulations, wrath, strife, seditions, heresies, Envyings, murders, drunkenness, Revellings, and much more. It is certainly un-holy, un-righteous and immoral. This is the nature of Anti-Christ.

The destiny of evil is total eradication from the face of the earth. The personification of evil in all its forms, whether human or spirit will be placed in the lake of fire for all eternity.

You may be thinking, "If evil is defeated, why are we Christians in a life and death battle with it? The answer is simple…because the devil has no power except that which we give him. He steals it from us with lies and suggestion that appeal to our own evil nature. Multiply this by billions of men, women, boys and girls and you amass lots of power. The devil takes all that power and rules through his captives.

Hear the words of Jesus on this wise…

"When the Son of man shall come in his glory, and all the holy angels with him, then shall he sit upon the throne of his glory: And before him shall be gathered all nations: and he shall separate them one from another, as a shepherd divides *his* sheep from the goats: And he shall set the sheep on his right hand, but the goats on the left. Then the King will say to those on his right, "Come, you who are blessed of my Father, inherit the kingdom prepared for you from the foundation of the world." Then shall he say also unto them on the left hand, "Depart from me, ye cursed, into everlasting fire, prepared for the devil and his angels:" Matthew 25:31-34 & 41

Are you a sheep or are you a goat? Your destiny depends upon your decision. It's time to decide. Being a sheep is to accept Jesus as Lord and Savior and allow him the privilege of sitting on the throne of your life.. That involves repenting of your sins, getting off the throne of your life and allowing Jesus his rightful place as your shepherd. Do it today and you'll be "Born Again" into the family of God.

What does all of this have to do with the end of the world? Simply this…God will destroy the earth with fervent heat to wipe out any remembrance of evil. It is his judgment upon the wicked. The time is fast approaching. Knowing this is the 1st step towards living in harmony with God, your creator. It is also the only way to overcome evil in your own life. You now know why the earth is to be destroyed.

CHAPTER TWO

THE BEAST WITHIN

THE POWERS OF DARKNESS SEEK total domination of the human race. They will stop at nothing to attain absolute power. Because Jesus defeated them with his death, burial and resurrection as the sacrifice for sin, they call upon the nature of sin now in power within mankind. This sinful nature is what I call, "The Beast Within."

I will attempt to paint a word picture of this beast that lives inside of us all, exposing its character, appetites and plans for the future. I will show its origin and destiny.

I will also reveal God's plan for his children in relationship to living in this world subject to the Beastly appitites that rule most of us today.

"And I stood upon the sand of the sea, and saw a beast rise up out of the sea, having seven heads and ten horns, and upon his horns ten crowns, and upon his heads the name of blasphemy." Revelation 13:1

The apostle John, the author of the book of Revelation, tells us about "The Beast" that will rise up out of the sea. Most theologians look at this from a spiritual perspective, not literal. The sea is looked at as the sea of humanity. The seven heads being evil kingdoms that oppose Christ and blaspheme God, and the 10 crowns that exalt the deeds of the flesh as mentioned in Galatians 5:19-20.

The War In Heaven

Revelation 12:7-12 King James Version (KJV)

" And there was war in heaven: Michael and his angels fought against the dragon; and the dragon fought and his angels, and prevailed not; neither was their place found any more in heaven. And the great dragon was cast out, that old serpent, called the devil, and Satan, which deceived the whole world: he was cast out into the earth, and his angels were cast out with him.

And I heard a loud voice saying in heaven, Now is come salvation, and strength, and the kingdom of our God, and the power of his Christ: for the accuser of our brethren is cast down, which accused them before our God day and night. And they overcame him by the blood of the Lamb, and by the word of their testimony; and they loved not their lives unto the death.

Therefore rejoice, ye heavens, and ye that dwell in them. Woe to the inhibitors of the earth and of the sea! For the devil is come down unto you, having great wrath, because he knoweth that he hath but a short time." Rev. 7:12 ff

The above verses tell us that there was a war between God and Satan. It took place in Heaven. Notice that Satan is also mentioned by several of his other names, that old serpent, the devil, the accuser of the brethren and the great dragon. We are told that he did not win the battle against the angel Michael and the armies of our God. As a result, he was thrown out of heaven. But God did not allow his enemy to roam the universe. He was cast down to the earth.

Here's what Jude had to say, "I will therefore put you in remembrance, though ye once knew this, how that the Lord, having saved the people out of the land of Egypt, afterward destroyed them that believed not. And the angels which kept not their first estate, but left their own habitation, he hath reserved in everlasting chains under darkness unto the judgment of the great day." Jude 5-6

Jesus said this, "And the seventy returned again with joy, saying, Lord, even the devils are subject unto us through thy name. And he said unto them, I beheld Satan, as lightning, fall from heaven." Luke 10: 17-18

So the war in heaven left God's enemy to be cast to earth where he and all of his angels, now demons, dwell. He knows that his time is short so he makes war on the saints to prevent them from experiencing God's love and blessings. All of this tells me that we are the objects of Satan's wrath. Peter backs this notion up in his letter I Peter 5:8, "Be sober, be vigilant; because your adversary the devil, as a roaring lion, walks about, seeking whom he may devour:" He says further that we are to resist him steadfast in the Faith and he will flee from us.

Herein is a picture of life on planet earth. We are the objects of the devil's wrath. He roams the earth, not Mars or another galaxy, seeking those who are unaware, unconcerned, and ignorant of the truth. When he finds them, he seeks to steal their peace, kill their dreams and destroy their souls.

So, on the one hand, we have a dragon after us attacking from a distance. But there is another enemy that hides inside of us. He is like the dragon in every way. He is, "The Beast Within."

The Origin of The Beast

The Beast was born out of jealousy and pride that led to disobedience. Its image and likeness is the same as the very character of the devil. He wanted to overthrow God and become God. ("I will ascend above the heights of the clouds; I will be like the most High." Isaiah 14:14) His original name was Lucifer when he served the

Most High God in heaven. It was he that waged war against God and led a third of the angels into the war in heaven. Chapter one gives all the other names that he goes by. He found himself on earth, with no power of his own. He had to steal that authority from man who had dominion over every living thing on the earth.

We were to take dominion and rule the planet under the authority and grace of God. But the serpent deceived Eve and talked Adam into disobeying God's command. The result of their actions caused spiritual death to both of them and allowed sin to enter into the hearts of men and pass on through every generation. Romans 5:12 and Genesis 2:15-17.

The Beast Invades Humanity

"Wherefore, as by one man sin entered into the world, and death by sin; and so death passed upon all men, for that all have sinned: (For until the law sin was in the world: but sin is not imputed when there is no law. Nevertheless death reigned from Adam to Moses, even over them that had not sinned after the similitude of Adam's transgression, who is the figure of him that was to come." Romans 5:12-14

Romans 5:18-21 tells us, "Therefore as by the offence of one *judgment came* upon all men to condemnation; even so by the righteousness of one *the free gift came* upon all men unto justification of life. For as by one man's disobedience many were made sinners, so by the obedience of one shall many be made righteous. Moreover the law entered, that the offence might abound. But where sin abounded, grace did much more abound: That as sin hath reigned unto death, even so might grace reign through righteousness unto eternal life by Jesus Christ our Lord."

So, Adam disobeyed God, just like Satan did and, like Satan, was thrown out of God's presence. Man falls from God's glorious presence into the darkness of sin. He lost the image and likeness of

God. But God still loves him and makes a plan for his restoration. Man would be justified by the blood of Jesus and His righteousness would be imparted to all who believe.

However, the sin that started with Satan filled the void in man's heart when God's Spirit departed. It's important to realize that God breathed into man, the breath of life and that was what made him a living soul. Life is always in relationship with God. If one is dead, he or she has no "breath of life" in them.

Adam possessed the, "Breath of Life" but it was taken away when he disobeyed. How do I know this? Because of Genesis 2:17 that says, "But of the tree of the knowledge of good and evil, thou shalt not eat of it: for in the day that thou eats thereof thou shalt surely die." He dies spiritually but ended up living as the walking dead lost in the darkness of sin.

We're all Zombies without the breath of life in us. Just in case you are still a bit confused, the "Breath of Life" is a reference to the Holy Spirit. His infilling is what causes us to be a living soul.

The Image & Likeness of The Beast

The image and likeness of the beast is exactly the same as Paul describes in Galatians 5 when discussing the works of the flesh. Hear again what he said, "Now the works of the flesh are manifest, which are these; adultery, fornication, uncleanness, lasciviousness, Idolatry, witchcraft, hatred, variance, emulations, wrath, strife, seditions, heresies, Envying, murders, drunkenness, rebelling, and such like: of the which I tell you before, as I have also told you in time past, that they which do such things shall not inherit the kingdom of God." Galatians 5:19-21

The above list is only a partial list. Paul ends the list with, "and such like" which means there are more but what has already been presented is enough to make his point. All of these attitudes live within us and are what paints a portrait of the "Beast Within"

We struggle with this evil nature every day. However, we were not the only ones. Hear what Paul said about himself, "For I know that in me (that is, in my flesh,) dwells no good thing: for to will is present with me; but how to perform that which is good I find not. For the good that I would I do not: but the evil which I would not, that I do." Romans 7:18-19 Paul goes on to say that by the grace of God he can find deliverance from the Beast.

This brings up a theological question. Am I a liar because I lie? Or do I lie because I am a liar at heart? Let's see what the scriptures say, "The heart is deceitful above all things, and desperately wicked: who can know it?" Jeremiah 17:9

Jesus said, "Not that which goes into the mouth defiles a man; but that which cometh out of the mouth, this defiles a man." Matthew 15:11

The nature of Sin, which entered the human race and passed upon all men, which is the image and likeness of Lucifer or Satan or the devil, whichever you want to call him, defiled mankind. Adam lost the image and likeness of his creator and now has to live with this evil beast inside that drives him to act out all manor of evil in the earth. Just so you know, Image and likeness are other words for character or nature.

We can easily see this being played out in our society. You see, those evening news reports do not report all the wonderful acts of righteousness. They rather inform us of who murdered who, who cheated on who, how many burglaries happened last night, what political deceptions were tossed to the media and so forth. Evil! Evil! And more Evil!

And what about the T.V. line-ups? The shows are the same, full of immorality, off color jokes, acts of violence and the like. It's hard to find a decent movie or sitcom without having to deal with bad language, violence, immorality or gay rights. We can clearly see the image and likeness of the Beast that lives within us. The work of the flesh is all around us. We are slaves to it and have no way out…or do we?

Overcoming The Beast

Paul tells the Galatians in chapter 5, "Stand fast therefore in the liberty wherewith Christ hath made us free, and be not entangled again with the yoke of bondage." "For we, through the Spirit, wait for the hope of righteousness by faith. For in Jesus Christ neither circumcision avails any thing, nor uncircumcision; but faith which works by love." "This I say then, Walk in the Spirit, and ye shall not fulfill the lust of the flesh. For the flesh lusts against the Spirit, and the Spirit against the flesh: and these are contrary the one to the other: so that ye cannot do the things that ye would. But if ye be led of the Spirit, ye are not under the law." (not under the law can be looked at as being not under the rule of the flesh or Beast.)

This is good news because it gives us two weapons that we can use to defeat the beast within. The above scripture says..

Wait for the hope of righteousness by Faith.

The hope of righteousness is a *state of mind*, in which we shall enjoy freedom from evil. This poor *body* will no more suffer from pain — but will be healthy, spiritual, powerful, and immortal. The soul will be no more tormented by sin, nor harassed with doubts, and fears — but will be holy, confident, and happy forever. Waiting for it means it is not here yet but is on its way.

This is the righteousness of God, which is by faith of Jesus Christ, unto all, and upon all, those who believe whether Jew or Gentile.

Seek to realize more of his presence, to feel more of his power, to experience more of his love, and to exhibit in your daily life and conversation more of his fruits. O my soul, see to it that this is your daily experience, and seek grace to say, "I, through the Spirit, wait for the hope of righteousness by faith." James Smith 1860

"This I say then, Walk in the Spirit, and ye shall not fulfill the lust of the flesh." Galatians 5:16

The quicker we allow the fruit of God's Spirit to manifest in us, the faster we will move away from the work of the flesh. We cannot hate if we are actively engaging in love. If we allow the peace of God to rule in our hearts, where is there room for anger or thoughts of hostility? If we cultivate the ability to suffer long (Longsuffering) where are critical attitudes and a domineering posture?

When we walk in the Spirit, we cannot walk in the flesh. We are given a free will choice as a Christian, to allow the image of God or allow the image of Satan to indwell us and reveal the likeness of the one we serve. We cannot serve them both. We have to reject one in order to serve the other. There is no neutrality.

Ok, I know what you will say next, **"How do I walk in the Spirit?"** *Answer:* 1st. get "Born Again" 2nd. Find out what the fruit of God's Spirit is. 3rd. Do not allow any emotions that are not the fruit to find their way into your thoughts, actions or dreams. The apostle Paul told the Ephesians to," Neither give place to the devil." Ephesians 4:27

Since the devil has placed his image and likeness inside of us and has in effect created a Beast, this scripture fits perfectly. We are told to give those deeds that come from the flesh, no place. To express it in a more dynamic way, we are not to give any place in our hearts and actions to the works of the flesh which are *these*; Adultery, fornication, uncleanness, lasciviousness, Idolatry, witchcraft, hatred, variance, emulations, wrath, strife, seditions, heresies, Envying, murders, drunkenness, revellings, and such like: of the which I tell you before, as I have also told *you* in time past, that they which do such things shall not inherit the kingdom of God. Galatians 5:19-21

We in effect, put the flesh to death when we give it no place. We take authority over the Beast by walking in the fruit of the Spirit which is, love, joy, peace, longsuffering, gentleness, goodness, faith, Meekness, temperance: against such there is no law. This is accomplished by faith, not our emotional state.

Life in the Spirit is a journey, and while there are many great passages throughout scripture that discuss the role and person of the Holy Spirit, Romans 8 is perhaps one of the best.

These two verses (Rom 8:26-27) are so rich and helpful in our lives in the Spirit.

1. The Spirit is searching our hearts and knows that we have a mind-set that is focused on him, even if we do not know exactly what we are supposed to pray.
2. The result is that our prayers are prayed 'according to the will of God' because the Holy Spirit is moving us thus to pray and is presenting the prayers that he is guiding us to pray to the Father.

Question? Where does that leave you? As we complete this chapter, have you realized anything? Maybe it's that you are part of a fallen race that has never been translated into the Jesus Generation. Maybe you now realize that you really are spiritually dead and want to be Born Again into the Kingdom of God's dear Son. If this is true, read these scriptures and ask Jesus to come into your heart.

John 3:16 "For God so loved the world, that he gave his only begotten Son, that whosoever believeth in him should not perish, but have everlasting life."

Are you a, **"Whosoever?"**

Romans 3:23 "For all have sinned, and come short of the glory of God;"

All means All, including you and me.

Romans 6:23, "For the wages of sin is death; but the gift of God is eternal life through Jesus Christ our Lord."

Death is inevitable but God has a gift for everyone who accepts Jesus. That gift is eternal life.

"I tell you, Nay: but, except [unless] ye repent, ye shall all likewise perish" **(Luke 13:3,5).**

"But now [God] commandeth [commands] all men everywhere to repent" **(Acts 17:30).**

The final decision is up to you. You can repent, turn from your wicked ways or those ways that are of the flesh and receive Jesus as your savior. He so loved you that he went to the cross as your substitute. He so loved you that he lived a life without sin so he could be the captain of your salvation. He is calling for you to come to him by faith in his finished work of grace.

CHAPTER THREE
THE DEVIL'S TOOLBOX

THE END OF THE WORLD is fast approaching and we are alive to possibly see it happen. As we wait for the signs of the times to emerge, we still need to walk by faith and keep ourselves from falling for the tricks of the devil. We can keep on keeping on by knowing what evil we face and how to fight against it.

The devil has a "Toolbox" full of tricks and devices that he uses against human beings and especially the children of God. Most folks are unaware of the "Wiles" of the devil. In fact, over 40% of Americans do not even believe that there is a real devil, only that he is a symbol for evil. (Pew Report)

The Bible tells us about his tricks. His purpose is to snare us with one or more of his tools thereby creating a, "Stronghold" in our lives, from which he can rule over us.

The literal meaning of a "Stronghold" is a fortified armed encampment that can be protected.

A "Snare" is a device or trap that is used to capture a prey. It can be a hunter's trap for small game or a net that is used to catch fish in the sea.

The purpose of tricks, snares, and other tools in "The Devil's Toolbox" is to capture you, and dominate your thoughts and actions with the ultimate goal of manifesting his evil character through you. Hear what Jesus said about the thief, as he referred to the devil.

"The thief cometh not, but for to steal, and to kill, and to destroy: I am come that they might have life, and that they might have it more abundantly." John 10:10

Whatever you call this, "Evil Being" you have to know, without a shadow of a doubt that he is real and he is after you to steal your dreams, kill any hope of happiness and destroy everything that is good in your life. He wants you dead but not before he torments you for a lifetime.

!!! News Flash !!!

The good news is that Jesus has defeated the devil and he has no power over you but what you give him. That's right, he has to get you to use your own "Free Will" to accept his lie. That's how he takes control. Let's see what the scriptures say so you know that I am not making this up.

"And having spoiled principalities and powers, he (Jesus) made a shew of them openly, triumphing over them in it." Colossians 2:5

Jesus spoiled all evil principalities and powers. That is a total defeat. Then he made an open shew…this denotes an old Roman picture of conquest over enemies. The evil king and leaders were tied by a rope to the back of a chariot and led down the middle of the city streets in a procession of conquest so everyone could see and laugh at the defeated foe. This is total victory.

Adam & Eve were not forced to submit to the devil when he was tempting them in the Garden of Eden. They had to engage their free will to do what the devil suggested. Take a read:

There's Always A Choice

The devil's power comes from your fleshly appetites. He has no power of his own. He must tap into your sinful nature and use it to accomplish his will. If you give him no place, he cannot do anything. He remains powerless.

We have already seen one tool that is in the devil's toolbox. It is, "The Lie" Jesus, speaking to some religious leaders of His day, said this…

"Ye are of your father the devil, and the lusts of your father ye will do. He was a murderer from the beginning, and abode not in the truth, because there is no truth in him. When he speaks a lie, he speaks of his own: for he is a liar, and the father of it." John 8"44

Lies That Kill, Steal & Destroy

How many times have we believed a lie? The politicians promise all kinds of things but never deliver. Are they lying? We believe their lies and then what?

Here are a few lies that the devil uses to cause us to do what he wants.

1. Drugs can't really hurt you. Try some and see for yourself.
2. Smoking is not really addictive.
3. Sex before marriage doesn't really hurt anyone.
4. Lying is ok as long as no one is hurt.
5. Taking a pen from work is not really stealing.
6. Drinking alcohol is ok. It's cool.

Now let's look at some other lies that are active in modern society.

Idology That Contradicts Bible Truth

The way you think is the basis for how you act and the way you live your life. There are certain lies that seek to alter your thought processes thereby changing your viewpoint. Here are a few:

There Is Only One True Church.

All the others are false. You must belong to our church in order to be saved. We are the true church of God.

This idology is so untrue. Salvation does not come as a result of a church membership. Nor does it come from a, "True Religion." It comes from the finished work of Jesus Christ on the cross. He paid the price of sin with His own blood. Hear what the scriptures say...

"Much more then, having now been justified by His blood, we shall be saved from the wrath of God through Him. For if while we were enemies we were reconciled to God through the death of His Son, much more, having been reconciled, we shall be saved by His life. And not only this, but we also exult in God through our Lord Jesus Christ, through whom we have now received the reconciliation." Romans 5:9-11

You Don't Have To Believe In Jesus To Attain Eternal Life.

The truth is, you do have to believe in Jesus to be saved and will not see heaven unless you accept him as Savior and Lord. Hear what was said to the people of Israel.

"Be it known unto you all, and to all the people of Israel, that by the name of Jesus Christ of Nazareth, whom ye crucified, whom God raised from the dead, even by him doth this man stand here before you whole. This is the stone, which was set at naught of you builders, which is become the head of the corner. Neither is there salvation in any other: for there is none other name under heaven given among men, whereby we must be saved." Acts 4:10-12

We Are All Children of God

Listen again to the scriptures. They reveal the truth.

"For as many as are led by the Spirit of God, they are the sons of God. For ye have not received the spirit of bondage again to fear;

but ye have received the Spirit of adoption, whereby we cry, Abba, Father.

If I Try To Be Good, That's Enough, Right? *The Spirit itself bears witness with our spirit, that we are the children of God:"* Romans 8:14

The Bible tells us that even religious leaders will not see God's kingdom unless they are, "Born Again" We must be, "Born Again" in order to see God's kingdom. That's what Jesus said. Keep reading!

"There was a man of the Pharisees, named Nicodemus, a ruler of the Jews: The same came to Jesus by night, and said unto him, Rabbi, we know that thou art a teacher come from God: for no man can do these miracles that thou doest, except God be with him. Jesus answered and said unto him, Verily, verily, I say unto thee, Except a man be born again, he cannot see the kingdom of God." John 3:3

There Are Many Ways To Heaven.

The lie is that we're all climbing the same mountain but by different paths. In other words, *there are many ways to attain eternal life.* This is in direct contrast to what Jesus said. Listen…

"Enter ye in at the strait gate: for wide is the gate, and broad is the way, that leads to destruction, and many there be which go in thereat:" Matthew 7:13

The narrow gate is Jesus. He said himself that…well, read it for yourself…

"Let not your heart be troubled: ye believe in God, believe also in me. In my Father's house are many mansions: if it were not so, I would have told you. I go to prepare a place for you. And if I go and prepare a place for you, I will come again, and receive you unto myself; that where I am, there ye may be also. And whither I

go ye know, and the way ye know. Thomas saith unto him, Lord, we know not whither thou goest; and how can we know the way? Jesus saith unto him, *I am the way, the truth, and the life: no man cometh unto the Father, but by me."* John 14:6

False Religions That Teaches Heracy

How often have you heard someone say. "It doesn't matter what religion you follow. You'll still end up in heaven." This lie extends to multi culturalism as well. People say it doesn't matter if you are Hindu, Muslim, Jew, Buddhist, Catholic–whatever. It's not a religion that saves us but rather a relationship with Jesus Christ.

There are many false religions in this world. I call some of them, "Isms." They teach heracy and lead people astray. They distort the truth, deny the diety of Christ and create a bondage that is very hard to break. Here are a few "Isms" to stay clear of. These are Anti-Christ.

Relativism – Relativism is the idea that there is no such thing as truth. The devil doesn't want you to believe in truth because if there is no truth, then there is also no right and wrong, and if there is no right and wrong, then anything goes. He can tempt you into sin much more easily if he can first get you to believe there is no such thing as sin. Relativism is everywhere in our society. It takes many different forms.

Under Relativism I can do my own thing. I can ignore any truth that does not line up with what I think. I am right all the time because there is no right or wrong, just whatever I want. This makes me my own god. How sad!

Utilitarianism – In Short…universalism is a theological doctrine that all human beings will eventually be saved: the principles and practices of a liberal Christian denomination founded in the 18th century originally to uphold the belief in "universal" salvation is now united with Unitarianism.

Here is the melting pot of all kinds of beliefs. You can believe anything you want and still be a member of this church because there is no standard or rule of practice, only what you think is right. The problem is…what we think is right is often wrong and with the devil lying to us; we can be easily misled unless we know God's truth. Jesus said…

"Take heed therefore that the light which is in thee be not darkness." Luke 11:35

Jesus knew that much of what was being presented as truth or light was not truth at all. It was actually darkness. We need to stay away from such as this.

Atheism - Atheism is defined as the disbelief or lack of belief in the existence of God. Whereas, Theism is the belief in the existence of a God, especially belief in one God as creator of the universe, intervening in it and sustaining a personal relation to his creatures.

This non-religion premise has in modern times become a religion unto itself. It denies God any place in reality and sets man up as his own god. The end of this can only be eternal death.

"There is a way which seems right unto a man, but the end thereof are the ways of death." Proverbs 14:12

Mormonism - The Mormon religion, (Mormonism), whose followers are known as Mormons and Latter Day Saints (LDS), was founded less than two hundred years ago by a man named Joseph Smith. He claimed to have received a personal visit from God the Father and Jesus Christ who told him that all churches and their creeds were an abomination. Joseph Smith then set out to begin a brand-new religion that claims to be the "only true church on earth.

This doctrine is a lie and a distortion of the truth. It is a humanistic approach to religion that denies the deity of Christ, The God Head, The Gifts of The Spirit and many other Bible norms.

Socialism - By the late 19th century, socialism emerged as "the most influential secular movement of the twentieth century, worldwide. It is a political ideology (or world view), a wide and divided political movement" Socialist parties and ideas remain a political force with varying degrees of power and influence on all continents. They head up national governments in many countries around the world.

Today, some socialists have also adopted the causes of other social movements, such as environmentalism, feminism and progressivism. They reject religion, faith and are anti-God

Satanism - is a group of ideological and philosophical beliefs based on Satan. Contemporary religious practice of Satanism began with the founding of the Church of Satan in 1966, although a few historical precedents exist.

Prior to the public practice, Satanism existed primarily as an accusation by various Christian groups toward perceived ideological opponents, rather than a self-identity. Satanism, and the concept of Satan, has also been used by artists and entertainers for symbolic expression.

Liberalism - Unlike traditional liberalism, there is a certain element of tyranny within the modern liberal movement. In past centuries, liberalism was used to literally liberate people from the rule of kings and tyrants.

Modern liberalism is now imposing its imoral beliefs on society. It is a forced movement that is functioning more like a tyranny than any other liberal beliefs have ever done. The premise of liberalism is mainly centered in anti-conservitiveism which rejects moral laws and respect for tradition.

The devil pushes liberalism more on the young, encouraging imoral behavior or anything that is anti-God.

Leagleism... (or nomism), in Messianic/Christian theology, is the act of putting the Law of Moses above the gospel, which is 1 Corinthians 15:1-4, by establishing requirements for salvation beyond faith (trust) in Jesus Christ, specifically, trust in His finished work - the shedding of his blood for our sins, and reducing the broad, inclusive, and general precepts of the Bible to narrow and rigid moral codes.

It is an over-emphasis of discipline of conduct, or legal ideas, usually implying an allegation of misguided rigour, pride, superficiality, the neglect of mercy, and ignorance of the grace of God or emphasizing the letter of law at the expense of the spirit.

Here are a few non "isms" but equally anti-God:

Witchcraft – This is the practice of magic or sorcery by anyone outside the religious mainstream of a society. This term is used in different ways in different times and places. Witchcraft is part of the Occult that deny God and rejects Jesus as Lord. It is centered in mysticism and preys on uniformed folks that seek spiritual answers.

Jehovah's Witness - The Jehovah's Witnesses are best known for going door-to-door. You have probably seen them in your area, and more than likely they have knocked on your door. They recently spent over 1.2 billion hours in one year proclaiming the so-called "good news of Jehovah and His Kingdom".

Jehovah's Witnesses reject the Trinity, believing Jesus to be a created being and the Holy Spirit to essentially be the inanimate power of God. Jehovah's Witnesses reject the concept of Christ's substitutionary atonement and instead hold to a ransom theory, that Jesus' death was a ransom payment for Adam's sin.

New Age - The **New Age** is a term applied to a range of spiritual or religious beliefs and practices that developed in Western nations during the 1970s. Precise scholarly definitions of the movement differ in their emphasis, largely as a result of its highly eclectic structure. Although analytically often considered to be religious, those involved in it typically prefer the designation of "spiritual" and rarely use the term "New Age" themselves. Many scholars of the subject refer to it as the **New Age movement**. It is very close to Universalism in that it believes in the spiritual but denied the truth of One God, One Lord and One Spirit, which is the centerpiece of Christianity.

Islam - "The source of the word, (Allah), who is the Islamic god, goes back to pre-Muslim times. Islam calls Allah god, which is not the God of the bible. Allah has about 1.6 billion followers worldwide. In 2010, Muslims made up 23.2% of the global population. According to the Encyclopedia of Religion, Allah corresponded to the Babylonian god Baal, and Arabs knew of him long before Mohammed worshipped him as the supreme god.

Before Islam, the Arabs recognized many gods and goddesses; each tribe had their own deity. There were also nature deities. Allah was the god of the local Quarish tribe, which was Mohammed's tribe before he invented Islam to lead his people out of their polytheism. Allah was then known as the Moon god, who had three daughters who were viewed as intercessors for the people.

Demonic Suggestions

We could go on and on but you get the point, right? There is a suggestion made by the devil that is a lie. It is presented as truth. If we believe it, we fall prey to the devil's manipulation and eventual take over. He wants to be the, "Voice In Your Head" that lord's over you. He wants to lead you away from all that is Godly. He wants to sit on God's throne which is in your heart.

All that has been mentioned above deal with lies that if accepted and believed will capture you and lead you from the light of God's glory into darkness.

Pitfalls In Personality…The Deeds of The Flesh

Now here are a few inward traps that cause sickness in our bodies and hasten our demise. These character flaws are used by the devil to capture us and take us down the broad road to destruction. They are a product of our own fallen nature. The Bible calls them the "Works of The Flesh." There is a full list in Galatians chapter five. I present them again because it is important that you know them and recognize them in you when they raise their evil heads.

"Now the works of the flesh are manifest, which are these; adultery, fornication, uncleanness, lasciviousness, Idolatry, witchcraft, hatred, variance, emulations, wrath, strife, seditions, heresies, envying, murders, drunkenness, revellings, and such like: of the which I tell you before, as I have also told you in time past, that they which do such things shall not inherit the kingdom of God." Galatians 5:19-21

All the devil has to do is to suggest a plan of action that involves one or more of these character flaws and if you buy it, you're off into the flesh that cannot please God. If he tells you that your brother's wife is sexy and you probably could have her and you start thinking of the reality of that encounter, you have committed adultery. Lust takes over and ego soars and imaginations rule. You don't have to do the act, just think about it.

The same is true of pornography. If you are just looking, it's still fornication in your mind and that will distort your sense of morality and steal your Godly values.

"But I say unto you, that whosoever looks on a woman to lust after her hath committed adultery with her already in his heart." Matthew 5:28

The devil doesn't make you do anything. He only suggests it and sometimes it can be a powerful illusion like he did with Jesus in the wilderness. It is your own will that takes you down the road to hell or resist him and go on in the Spirit.

The Bible says that Satan, (the devil) is the accuser of the brethren. Here is the exact scripture...

"And I heard a loud voice saying in heaven, Now is come salvation, and strength, and the kingdom of our God, and the power of his Christ: for the accuser of our brethren is cast down, which accused them before our God day and night. And they overcame him by the blood of the Lamb, and by the word of their testimony; and they loved not their lives unto the death." Revelation 12:10-11

The, "They" in Verse 11 is us, The Brethren. We can and do overcome this accuser with The Blood of The Lamb, The Word of Our Testimony and Because We Loved Not Our Lives Unto Death. See?...we can have victory.

You may be wondering what types of accusations are made against us. Here are a few:

1. You are ugly and stupid.
2. You are not worthy of anyone's love.
3. You cannot be saved because you have done too many bad things.
4. You are a bad person so go ahead and be bad.
5. And so on

Demonic accusations are meant to cause doubt, fear, low self-esteem and worry among other things. However, the scripture (Revelation 12:11) also says that the accusation is against you before the throne of God. He accuses you in front of all the host of heaven. All the things you do wrong are brought before the court of God's Justice. He is constantly telling God how bad you are. If we are "Born Again" Jesus, who is seated at the right hand of God, The Father, is interceding on our behalf, saying in effect, "He or she is mine. Their names are written in the Lamb's Book of Life. They've been washed in my Blood."

Watch Out For These

Temptation... Satan nags us to act on addictive urges and to entertain selfishness and greed. How can we resist this direct temptation? Jesus used a two-step defensive technique: first, he ordered Satan to leave; then he quoted scripture. You have the right to tell Satan to leave when you are confronted with temptation. There is great power in memorizing scripture, as Jesus did. Scripture power not only intimidates Satan, but it also brings the Spirit of God into your heart. Listen again to the scriptures...

"There hath no temptation taken you but such as is common to man: but God is faithful, who will not suffer you to be tempted above that ye are able; but will with the temptation also make a way to escape, that ye may be able to bear it". *I Corinthians 10:*

Deception... The devil has been called "the great deceiver." He attempts to counterfeit every true principle the Lord presents. Although Satan will lie to you, you can count on the Spirit of God to tell you the truth. That's why the gift of the Holy Ghost is so essential.

Contention... Satan is the father of contention. He delights in seeing good people argue. When there is contention in your home or workplace, immediately stop whatever you are doing and seek to make peace. It doesn't matter who started it.

"Be not hasty in thy spirit to be angry: for anger rests in the bosom of fools." Ecclesiastes 7:9

We do not want to be counted with the fools of this world. However, the devil wants us there so he and the rest of the inhabitants of planet earth can laugh at us.

Discouragement... Satan effectively uses this tool on the most faithful Saints when all else fails. President Ezra Taft Benson (1899–1994) gave suggestions for fighting discouragement. They include serving others; working hard and avoiding idleness; practicing good health habits; seeking a priesthood blessing; listening to inspiring music; counting your blessings; and setting goals and above all, as the scriptures teach, we are to pray always.

When we get discouraged, it is usually because we didn't get our way. Something hindered us from being on top. Instead, we got fired, lost in a card game, watched as our spouse left us, or some other bad thing.

There is an easy remedy for discouragement. That is to make Jesus the Lord of your life and trust him in every circumstance. This takes the burden of responsibility off of you and allows God to work out everything for good. (See Romans 8:28)

Situational Ethics That Replaces Absolute Truth

This is another name for moral relativism. The idea is that nothing is right or wrong except for the intentions and circumstances of the moral choice. If you mean well and the circumstances justify it, then what you've chosen to do is okay. Huge numbers of Christians have accepted this premise to justify abortion. If it feels right, it must be ok. However, feeling right is not the same as God's Moral Laws. His Word is absolute, no matter what you or I feel.

The devil will always invoke a situational ethic into the mix so as to divert our thinking away from the absolute truth of God's Word. Here's an example of situational sin…

Scientific Facts That Contradict Biblical Revelation

This is the idea that the only kind of truth is scientific truth. It's a powerful lie of Satan because it is one of those things, which is simply assumed in society.

"We all know that science has disproved the Bible right?" Wrong.

All truth is God's truth and true science is always the sister of true theology. Scientism is an offshoot of atheism. "There is no God. There are just the laws of science. That's all." No! No! No! That's wrong.

This Godless doctrine ushered in evolution back in the 18th century. It was the devil's way of offering a believable platform for those who did not want to follow God. As you may know, this theory says we evolved over millions of years into what we are today, with no divine influences. Thus we are our own gods and masters of our own destinies. Hitler used this theory to killed six million Jews in WWII. African Americans were once considered sub-standard beings because of this theory. Hear what the Bible says...

"And as it is appointed unto men once to die, but after this the judgment: So Christ was once offered to bear the sins of many; and unto them that look for him shall he appear the second time without sin unto salvation." Hebrews 9:27-28 We should be looking to Jesus, not science.

False Prophets & Teachers

Here's what the Bible says about false prophets and teachers...

"And many false prophets shall rise, and shall deceive many." Matthew 24:11 Mark 13:22 says it this way..."For false Christs and false prophets shall rise, and shall shew signs and wonders, to seduce, if *it were* possible, even the elect."

It is clear that the goal of these false prophets is to deceive. Their teachings are false. Their efforts are for self-empowerment. Their doctrines are demonic in nature. Have you ever heard of Rev. Jones that took his congregation overseas and killed them all... but only after abusing the females and stealing their wealth?

Let's bring this on the level of the average Christian who can also be a false teacher. Here again what Jesus said to His disciples...

"For many shall come in my name, saying, I am Christ; and shall deceive many.: Matthew 24:5

The term, "Christ" literally means Anointed. What is really being said is that there will be many that claim to be anointed of God, like Jesus was anointed. This is the mark of a Christian but these false Christians are not anointed. They just claim to be. They will be able to talk the talk but do not follow the truth of the gospel message. A good example is the Mormon Church. These days they claim to be the Latter Day Saints and call themselves Christians. However, they believe very differently. Their doctrines are anti-Christ. These false believers are sprinkled throughout all main line denominations.

How many folks do you know that profess to be a Christian but have no knowledge of what it really means? Some even claim to be anointed when they operate in the flesh and promote a secular gospel that is a kin to Humanism.

Sickness & Disease

The devil will use sickness and disease to steal our strength, destroy our health and kill our healthy cells. However, we are challenged to believe another report. This time it's not the doctor's diagnosis but the Word of God.

The question is, **"Does God Want You To Be Healed"** or **Will He Say No To Your Plea?** I was a Baptist, way back when. Our prayer for healing always started with, **"If It Be Thy Will"** We never knew if it was God's will to heal or not. Maybe there was a reason why He didn't want us to be healed. Then I looked into the scriptures and found these declarations:

Healed By His Stripes

- *"He is despised and rejected of men; a man of sorrows, and acquainted with grief: and we hid as it were our faces from him; he was despised, and we esteemed him not. Surely he hath borne our griefs, and carried our sorrows: yet we did esteem him stricken, smitten of God, and afflicted. But he was wounded for our transgressions, he was bruised for our iniquities: the chastisement of our peace was upon him; and with his stripes we are healed." Isaiah 5.:3-6* "Who hath believed our report? and to whom is the arm of the Lord revealed?" Isaiah 53:1

Note: This suffering servant, spoken of by Isaiah, has borne our grief and carried our sorrows. He was stricken of God. He was wounded for our transgressions and bruised for our iniquities. The chastisement of our peace was upon him....*and With His Stripes We Are Healed.*

The only person that qualifies in all these areas is Jesus. Isaiah clearly said that our healing is in His stripes, which were the beatings and burses and wounds. His blood and subsequent death brought healing to those who believed his report.

Healed By The Prayer of Faith

- "Is anyone among you sick? Let them call the elders of the church to pray over them and anoint them with oil in the name of the Lord. And the prayer offered in faith will make the sick person well; the Lord will raise them up. If they have sinned, they will be forgiven." James 5:14-15

Healed Through Worship

- "Worship the LORD your God, and his blessing will be on your food and water. I will take away sickness from among you…" Exodus 23:25

Healed By The Lord, Just Because

- "But I will restore you to health and heal your wounds,' declares the LORD" Jeremiah 30:17

- "I have seen their ways, but I will heal them; I will guide them and restore comfort to Israel's mourners, creating praise on their lips. Peace to those far and near," says the LORD. "And I will heal them." Isaiah 57:18-19

Healing By God's Divine Will

- "He himself bore our sins" in his body on the cross, so that we might die to sins and live for righteousness; "by his stripes (wounds) you were healed." 1 Peter 2:24

- "He gives strength to the weary and increases the power of the weak." Isaiah 40:29

- "Then they cried to the LORD in their trouble, and he saved them from their distress. He sent out his word and healed them; he rescued them from the grave. Let them give thanks to the LORD for his unfailing love and his wonderful deeds for mankind." Psalms 107:19-21

- "He heals the brokenhearted and binds up their wounds." Psalms 147:3

- "Jesus went through all the towns and villages, teaching in their synagogues, proclaiming the good news of the kingdom and healing every disease and sickness." Matthew 9:35

The Devil Uses Sickness & Diseases To Oppress The Children of God

The Bible tells us *"How God anointed Jesus of Nazareth with the Holy Ghost and with power: who went about doing good, and healing all that were oppressed of the devil; for God was with him."*.

"And when they came to the crowd, a man came up to him and, kneeling before him, said, "Lord, have mercy on my son, for he has seizures and he suffers terribly. For often he falls into the fire, and often into the water. And I brought him to your disciples, and

they could not heal him." And Jesus answered, "O faithless and twisted generation, how long am I to be with you? How long am I to bear with you? Bring him here to me." And Jesus rebuked the demon and it came out of him, and the boy was healed instantly" Matthew 17:14-18

Is there any question as to God not wanting his children to be healed? There wasn't a time when someone did not get healed. Sometimes it was because they asked to be healed. Other times God just healed them.

We should never say, "If It Be Thy Will." Based upon these scriptures, we should now know that it is and always will be God's will that we be healed.

Why Then, In Our Day, Do Many Sick Folk Not Get Healed?

That is a good question. I have prayed for some and seen them receive their healing. I have also prayed and saw nothing happen. Here's what I have surmised after more than 60 years of following Christ.

Some folks just do not believe that Jesus can or will heal them. Some have more faith in doctors and pills than they do in Jesus. Some secretly like their condition because they get sympathy and attention that they would ordinarily not get if they were well. Some get disability checks and do not have to work and like it that way. Some are reaping what they sowed and have to endure it. Some are weak in faith and lose hope before they are healed. I remember the words of Jesus. He said, "Be it unto you according to your faith." Matthew 9:29

Still others just do not get healed and do not know why. They pray, they cry, they plead and nothing happens. The woman with the issue of blood was bound for 18 years. The blind man was blind from birth so God's power could be used to glorify the name of

Jesus. Sometimes there are reasons why things don't go, as we so desire.

This one thing I do know…It is God's will that all of us be in good health and prosper. Until He tells me otherwise, I will continue to seek him for my healing and believe that I have what I ask for. In fact, I regularly call forth healing into existence. It is an unseen reality that is and is not but will soon be.

Sickness can come upon us from several sources. If we smoke and get lung cancer, it is our fault, not the devil's or even God's. If we drink alcohol in excess and become an alcoholic, whose fault is it? If we work ourselves to death and come down with a cold or get sick, is it anyone's fault other than our own?

In a world tainted by sin, sickness and disease will always be with us, at least until Jesus comes again. We are fallen beings, with physical bodies prone to disease and illness. Some sickness is simply a result of the natural course of things in this world. Sickness can also be the result of a demonic attack. However, sickness does not originate with God.

The Bible, again says, *"The Lord is not slack concerning his promise, as some men count slackness; but is longsuffering to us-ward,* **not willing that any should perish,** *but that all should come to repentance."* 2 Peter 3:9

If God does not want us to perish, that is a clear indication that he does not afflict us with a sicknesses or a disease that would cause our demise. It's just not logical.

I believe I have made a good case against, "If It Be Thy Will". All these scriptures lead me to one big conclusion…It is God's will that we be healed and stay in good health.

Expectations That Discourage "Free Will" Choices

The devil often uses people to do his bidding. It could be a parent, co-worker, teacher or even a friend. Their efforts to impose expectation on you can be very painful. It could be an immoral act, a restrictive influence or even a command that goes against what you feel is right.

This type of expectation puts pressure on you to be or do what they want instead of what you feel is right. It is a form of oppression.

On the other hand, God's expectations are designed to give you the greatest freedom and blessings possible. Hear what the psalmist said many years ago, *"My soul, wait thou only upon God; for my expectation is from him."* Psalm 62:5

If you feel that what others are expecting of you is not in God's plan for your life or that you just do not have peace about what is expected of you, reject it, no matter who it is. Your peace is more important than their expectations. That will keep the devil at bay and you free. We should always look for what God would expect of us and reject the expectations of others. By the way, God's expectations are clearly revealed in the Bible.

Illusions & Mind Games That Confuse And Manipulate

The devil will also use illusions to confuse you or cause you to think that he has power over you or cause you to think that he owns the world and even the people in it. Listen to how he tried to trick Jesus…

"The devil said to him, (Jesus), "I will give you all the power and glory of these kingdoms. All of it has been given to me, and I give it to anyone I please." Luke 4:6

The devil did not own the kingdoms of the world. Nor did he have the power and glory of those kingdoms. They belong to God. *"The earth is the Lord's, and the fullness thereof; the world, and they that dwell therein. For he hath founded it upon the seas, and established it upon the floods." Psalm 24:1-2*

As the story goes, the devil took Jesus up to the pinnacle of the temple to show him all the kingdoms of the world. The problem is, you cannot see all the kingdoms of the world from that vantage point.

The devil likes to play with your mind and manipulate your imagination. He will play mind games with you in hopes that you will engage your imagination to mentally see what is being suggested. It all takes place in the mind and it is usually a bold faced lie.

Here's how it works with folks today. A thought enters the mind from the devil or one of his demons. The thought is an image of a kid in a store looking at a toy truck. The suggestion is, "Take it, no one is looking. The kid mentally sees himself playing with it and sees all his friends being envious of him because he has the new truck and they do not... so he steals it. The kid is you and your feelings are fully engaged.

It could be a lonely guy wishing he could find a girl. Suddenly a thought enters his mind. It's of an old girlfriend. Another thought tells him, "Boy I could really ...*you can fill in the rest*. Now he is mentally engaged in a sexual act that is not real...thus, he falls into sin, gets depressed because he realizes he is still alone, hates himself for thinking that way and becomes suicidal.

The devil will always suggest that you picture things that you don't or cannot have. He does this because it is tormenting and he loves to torment us as he takes us down the road to hell. His ultimate goal is to drive you to a place where you will act out your fantasies. Thus comes rape, murder, watching pornography and all the deeds of the flesh listed in Galatians chapter five..

The thing to realize is...*not all of our thoughts are ours*. We get some from the devil, from our own sinful nature and even some from the Holy Spirit. We have to try the spirits to be sure they are from God before we act on them. Hear what the apostle John says...

"Beloved, believe not every spirit, but try the spirits whether they are of God: because many false prophets are gone out into the world. Hereby know ye the Spirit of God: Every spirit that confesses that Jesus Christ is come in the flesh is of God: And every spirit that confesses not that Jesus Christ is come in the flesh is not of God: and this is that spirit of antichrist, whereof ye have heard that it should come; and even now already is it in the world." I John 4:1-5

Jesus used the scriptures to defeat the devil. He said, **"IT IS WRITTEN."** He knew the Word of God and used it to put down the lie and dispel the illusion. This means if we want to defeat the devil, we also need to know what is written so we can use it at the appropriate time. I am referring to the written Word of God, the Bible. If we are tempted to steal, we can say, it is written, *"Thou Shalt Not Steal"* Exodus 20:15 This will dispel the illusion. Then we can tell the devil to take a hike.

Knowing scripture is essential to winning the battle. Here's what Paul said to the Corinthian church back in the first century, *"For the weapons of our warfare are not carnal but mighty in God for pulling down strongholds, casting down imaginations and every high thing that exalts itself above the knowledge of God, bringing every thought into captivity to the obedience of Christ"* II Corinthians 10:4-5

If we know the scripture, we can cast down every imagination that is against the knowledge of God. That is what Jesus did. He knew that God said that man was not to steal and he used that truth to overcome the devil.

Remember, what God did in the Old Testament was then. We are now in a New Covenant where God's grace (Unmerited Favor) rules the day. God does not punish his children with disease or sickness. His loving hand is extended towards all who believe. He wants them all to come to repentance.

I am sure you will find other tools that should be added to the devil's toolbox. I have shown you enough to open your eyes to the, "Wiles" of the devil in hopes that you search out ways to defend yourself. We are in a fight for our lives that has eternal consequences.

The apostle Peter gave us a clear and present danger with an assurance of victory. Here's what he said, *"Be sober, be vigilant; because your adversary the devil, as a roaring lion, walks about, seeking whom he may devour: Whom resist stedfast in the faith, knowing that the same afflictions are accomplished in your brethren that are in the world." I Peter 5:8-9*

The apostle John leaves us with this…*"And now, little children, abide in him; that, when he shall appear, we may have confidence, and not be ashamed before him at his coming." I John 2:28*

CHAPTER FOUR

DEAD MEN WALKING

You'll never guess what happened to me while waiting for this world to end. I realized that I am living among the walking dead. I couldn't believe that the people around me were all dead but still walking around talking and fighting with each other.

We Christians walk among the living dead. We even at times bond with them and adopt their values. This is all happening as we wait for the end of the world to come. It is the norm in most countries.

The world, at least America, has a strange fascination about dead people. We have a TV show called "The Walking Dead" and movies that are promoted with such phrases as, "I See Dead People."

Filmmakers are trying to tap into a lust for horror and evil that wells up in the hearts of men. Skulls are more prevalent on T-Shirts. Body art has a full display of "All Things Dead" tattoos. Suicide is more prevalent than ever.

Righteousness in the hearts of men and women is being replaced with unrighteousness. There is a huge swing from right to left in the morality of Americans. This is so obvious in these last days than ever before. It's like the end of the world has fallen upon us.

Who would have ever thought that a political party would openly support Abortion, Gay Rights, and other immoral lifestyles? Who would have ever thought that Socialism would grow in popularity in the land of the free and the brave?

The Source of The Problem

The problem, as I see it, is the condition of man's heart. He is utterly depraved and wicked at the core. Read what the Bible has to say…

"The heart is deceitful above all things, and desperately wicked: who can know it?" Jeremiah 17:9

Deceitful and *Desperately Wicked*…this is a picture of the heart. Jesus embellished this condition when he said, *"Not that which goes into the mouth defiles a man; but that which cometh out of the mouth, this defiles a man." Matthew 15:11*

So we cannot blame our shortcomings on our society, our parents, our environment, a schoolteacher, poverty, or anything else…except ourselves. Our belief system and our actions shape our society. It's not the other way around.

This fascination with "Death" is already in our hearts. We lust for it and even wear it in public on clothing and promote it in our speech. As Christians, we realize that our hearts are or were of the same mindset but we no longer desire to participate in the death of a nation and/or the loss of even one human soul. Some of us have read the scriptures and are even now seeking to apply its divine truth. We are counseled by God and do not put our will above his. He tells us such things as this;

"Keep thy heart more than anything that is guarded; for out of it are the issues of life." Proverbs 4:23

To keep one's heart is to guard it so it doesn't get stolen, damaged or overwhelmed by evil. The practical "How To" knowledge on what exactly to do is written on the pages of the scriptures in nuggets of wisdom and pearls of instruction that are given to us as precious promises.

The Bible looks at life, as a state of being that is Spiritual, not physical. Life is always in relationship to God. Abundant life, as Jesus said in John 10:10 is the full expression and flow of God dwelling with man in a blessed relationship. The heart of man is the throne of God. We are his temple. *"now ye not that ye are the temple of God, and that the Spirit of God dwells in you? If any man defile the temple of God, him shall God destroy;"* I Corinthians 3:16-17

Death, on the other hand is viewed in biblical terms as a separation from God; a banishment; a total and complete rejection by God; and being cut off from the presence of God forever.

Physical death is only a transition into the spiritual realm where souls are judged and assigned an eternal destiny. Hear what the Bible says;

"The soul that sinneth, it shall die" Ezekiel 18:20... this is not a maybe but an absolute. You sin, you die and death is not only physical but also spiritual. The soul is forever separated from the presence of a holy and righteous God.

The Biblical Meaning of Sin

Let's take a moment to clarify the biblical meaning of SIN. The original meanings of *sin* were largely concerned with religious matters ("an offense against religious or moral law"; "a transgression of the law of God"; "a vitiated state of human nature in which the self is estranged from God"), as they still are today.

In a religious context, sin is an act of transgression against divine law. Sin can also be viewed as any thought or action that endangers the ideal relationship between an individual and God.

When we sin, we engage in an act of rebellion against the known laws of God. It can be a conscious act or as a result of a lack of knowledge as to the law. It's like being stopped for speeding, only to discover that the speed limit was 35 and you thought it was 45. The law is still the law. The fact that you did not know it doesn't matter. You are still guilty.

So it is with God. His mark is moral purity, which is holiness. To not know or to know and not be holy is still Sin and God has said that you are guilty and has already passed judgment on all who sin. That soul or all those souls shall die.

Sin pollutes the heart, making it evil and rebellious. The heart, that was originally created to love God and to manifest His image and likeness in the earth, has become carnal which the Bible calls, "The Flesh".... These are the, **"Dead Men Walking."** They miss the mark of holiness, falling short of what God intended for them. They walk in the flesh, in darkness and are dead spiritually. This applies to everyone that has not been "Born Again" on the earth. They are, "Dead Men Walking"

The works of this "Flesh" known as carnality, has already been discussed.

Two Men & Their Descendants

The Bible tells the story of two men and follows their descendants through history. These two men were prototypes. One man was Adam. His descendants will all die because of Sin. However the other man is Jesus and his descendants will live forever. Read what Paul says to the church at Corinth and the church at Rome:

"For as in Adam all die, even so in Christ shall all be made alive. But every man in his own order: Christ the firstfruits; afterward they that are Christ's at his coming. I Corinthians 15:22-23

All die in Adam. Why?

"Wherefore, as by one man, sin entered into the world and death by sin; and so death passed upon all men, for that all have sinned:

Nevertheless death reigned from Adam to Moses, even over them that had not sinned after the similitude of Adam's transgression, who is the figure of him that was to come." Romans 5:12 &14

All Made Alive In Christ. How?

Jesus spoke to the crowd around him and said, *"For God so loved the world, that he gave his only begotten Son, that whosoever believeth on him should not perish, but have eternal life. ...* For God loved the world in this way: He gave his one and only Son, so that everyone who believes in him will not perish but have eternal life." John 3:16

It is important to know that the descendants of Adam were born of the flesh. Whereas those made alive in Christ were, "Born Again", of the Spirit.

"Jesus answered, Verily, verily, I say unto thee, except a man be born of water and of the Spirit, he cannot enter into the kingdom of God. That which is born of the flesh is flesh; and that which is born of the Spirit is spirit." John 3:5-6

Born of The Flesh

When the Bible speaks of the "flesh," it is often referring to our natural sin tendencies. We are all born with a sin nature (Romans 5:12). Our natural predilection is to please ourselves any way we see fit. We can be trained to behave in more socially acceptable ways and even find enjoyment in being kind to others.

However, without the power of God, we remain self-centered. We do what we do, even good things, because we receive some selfish payoff. Anything not done from faith or love for God; any deed not empowered by the Holy Spirit is a "work of the flesh" (Romans 8:8; 14:23).

Born of The Spirit

Those born of the Spirit are the descendants of Christ....in that they are now "In Christ". The Bible expresses it this way, *"I am crucified with Christ: nevertheless I live; yet not I, but Christ lives in me: and the life which I now live in the flesh, I live by the faith of the Son of God, who loved me, and gave himself for me."* Galatians 2:20

The First & Last Adam

"So it is written: "The first man, Adam, became a living being" the last Adam, a life-giving spirit. The spiritual did not come first, but the natural, and after that the spiritual. The first man was of the dust of the earth, the second man from heaven. As was the earthly man, so are those who are of the earth; and as is the man from heaven, so also are those who are of heaven. I Corinthians 15:45-48

Think of it this way. There were only two men that walked the earth that did not posses a sin nature. They were Adam, before he transgressed God's command and Jesus. All the rest of us possessed a sin nature at birth and are in bondage to it all of our lives.

So what does all of this have to do with "Dead Men Walking?" Only this… all the descendants of Adam, that being every human being that was born on the earth, throughout all the centuries, were born dead. They did not have the Spirit of God in them that was given to Adam at his creation. Death (Spiritual Separation from God), passed upon all men.

The dead men walking operate solely in their own flesh, which is a sinful or carnal nature. By nature, they transgress the laws of God, rebelling against his wisdom and counsel. It is their way or the highway. They are under the judgment of God at birth and are in need of a savior.

These folks formed nations, spoke different languages and developed different cultures, all without God. Doesn't this sound like our present day world? It is full of dead men and women walking in the flesh, ignoring the will of God, and living in a nature that is unholy, immoral, and rebellious towards the love of God.

It amazes me to read John 3:16. I cannot imagine how God could love a world in such a state of rebellion and to send his only Son to be a willing sacrifice for sin, which was the penalty that God himself imposed upon all souls that sin, especially knowing all would sin. What kind of love is this? It is glorious in our sight.

Who Are The Dead Men Walking?

Now that you know that everyone that has ever lived on planet earth, with the exception of those that have been "Born Again" are all Dead Men Walking…. how do you feel about that? We were also among the dead men walking in times past, until we were born again.

I am, "Born Again" and I feel great. I thank God every day that he sent Jesus as my substitute to die in my stead and to live the life I could not attain…all of this so I could be forgiven and redeemed from the curse of the law. What do you say? Email me at johnmarinelli@embarqmail.com and let me know what you think and how you feel.

The people of earth struggle in the darkness of their own sin, searching for life but see no value in living it because they know death is imminent and all their efforts will have been in vain. They question where they came from, why they are here and where they are going when they die.

I hope that this chapter has shined a light into your darkness and revealed a path that will lead you out of that darkened state of mind into the glorious light of God's forgiveness and love. This is the place where you can live and move and have your being. You can find yourself in him. This is the refuge where you can hide until Jesus comes again or we go to be with him.

I FIND MYSELF IN GOD

I find myself in God.
He is my, "Everything."
I know that He is Lord,
My life, my Hope, and King.

I find myself in God,
Not the ways of sin.
Nor do I look to others,
To know who I really am.

I find myself in God,
To whom I bow on bended knee.
He alone is my joy and strength
And where I want to be.

Written By
John Marinelli

CHAPTER FIVE

PORTRAIT OF THE DAMNED

"For the wrath of God is revealed from heaven against all ungodliness and unrighteousness of men, who hold the truth in unrighteousness;" Romans 1:1

FTER READING THIS SCRIPTURE, IT is apparent, to me anyway, that those who hold the truth in unrighteousness will no doubt face the wrath of God.

This chapter is designed to shed light on these kinds of people. Who are they? Where do they live? Why do they knowingly resist God? Are they really going to be damned by God? What does "Damned" mean? What exactly is the wrath of God? Will their damnation come now or when the end of the world happens?

We will search for the answers to the above questions using the KJV version of the Bible, beginning in Romans chapter One. Let's begin with some definitions so we know the biblical meanings.

A Few Definitions

What is the Biblical understanding of the wrath of God?

Wrath is defined as "the emotional response to perceived wrong and injustice," often translated as "anger," "indignation," "vexation," or "irritation." Both humans and God express wrath. But there is a vast difference between the wrath of God and the wrath of man. God's wrath is holy and always justified; man's is never holy and rarely justified.

In the Old Testament, the wrath of God is a divine response to human sin and disobedience. Idolatry was most often the occasion for divine wrath. Psalm 78:56-66 describes Israel's idolatry. The wrath of God is consistently directed towards those who do not follow his will (Deuteronomy 1:26-46; Joshua 7:1; Psalm 2:1-6). The Old Testament prophets often wrote of a day in the future, the "day of wrath" (Zephaniah 1:14-15). God's wrath against sin and disobedience is perfectly justified because his plan for mankind is holy and perfect, just as God himself is holy and perfect. God provided a way to gain divine favor—repentance—which turns God's wrath away from the sinner. To reject that perfect plan is to reject God's love, mercy, grace and favor and incur his righteous wrath.

The New Testament also supports the concept of God as a God of wrath who judges sin. The story of the rich man and Lazarus speaks of the judgment of God and serious consequences for the unrepentant sinner (Luke 16:19–31). John 3:36 says, "Whoever believes in the Son has eternal life, but whoever rejects the Son will not see life, for God's wrath remains on him." The one who believes in the Son will not suffer God's wrath for his sin, because the Son took God's wrath upon himself when he died in our place on the cross (Romans 5:6–11). Those who do not believe in the Son, who do not receive him as Savior, will be judged on the day of wrath (Romans 2:5–6).

The wrath of God is a fearsome and terrifying thing. Only those who have been covered by the blood of Christ, shed for us on the cross, can be assured that God's wrath will never fall on them. "Since we have now been justified by his blood, how much more shall we be saved from God's wrath through him!" (Romans 5:9).... Definition and copy taken from GotQuestions.org.

Damned By God

It is logical to assume that anyone that is under the wrath of God is also damned of God. However, what exactly does that mean? Here's what the dictionary says.

A damned human "in damnation" is said to be either in hell, or living in a state wherein they are divorced from heaven and/or in a state of disgrace from God's favor.

The KJV Bible Dictionary says this about the word "Damn."

1. To sentence to eternal torments in a future state; to punish in hell.
2. To condemn; to decide to be wrong or worthy of punishment; to censure; to reprobate.
3. To condemn; to explode; to decide to be bad, mean, or displeasing, be hissing or any mark of disapprobation; as, to damn a play, or a mean author.
4. A word used in profaneness; a term of execration.

We should never say, "Damn You" because it calls for the wrath of God to be upon that individual and seeks a final solution of eternal damnation. We should not wish that on even our worst enemy. Besides, it is not our job to be the judge, jury and executioner over anyone. That is God's responsibility.

Why Would God Condemn or Damn Anyone?

God has gone to great lengths to reveal himself to mankind. We are without excuse when it comes to acknowledging the existence of God.

"Because that which may be known of God is manifest in them; for God hath shewed it unto them, For the invisible things of him from the creation of the world are clearly seen, being understood by the things that are made, even his eternal power and Godhead; so that they are without excuse:" Romans 1:19

God has a specific reason to pour out his wrath and even damn the souls of men to an eternal death. Here it is, straight from the Word of God.

"Because that, when they knew God, they glorified him not as God, neither were thankful; but became vain in their imaginations, and their foolish heart was darkened. Professing themselves to be wise, they became fools, And changed the glory of the uncorruptible God into an image made like to corruptible man, and to birds, and four-footed beasts, and creeping things." Romans 1:21-23

Man has always known that there was a God that created him and ruled over his universe. However, to deny God's existence and refuse to glorify him as God comes with consequences.

"Wherefore God also gave them up to uncleanness through the lusts of their own hearts, to dishonor their own bodies between themselves: Who changed the truth of God into a lie, and worshipped and served the creature more than the Creator, who is blessed for ever. Amen...For this cause God gave them up unto vile affections:" Romans 1:24-26a

> **Vile Affections...** The descent into evolutionary paganism is always soon followed by gross immorality, specifically including sexual perversion, such as described in Romans 1:26-29. Ancient Sodom was so notorious for homosexuality that its practice has long been known as sodomy (see Genesis 13:13; 19:4-9). The practice became so widespread in ancient Greece that it was considered normal and even desirable. Other examples are abundant and, of course, it is quickly becoming accepted—even encouraged—here in America. Not surprisingly, this was preceded by widespread return to evolutionism in science and education.
>
> *(Institute For Creation Research)*

Vile Affections

When God gives up on you, you fall into vile affections and become the worst of the worst among human beings. Here's a list of vile affections: Romans 1:27-

1. **Going Against Nature**...*for even their women did change the natural use into that which is against nature.* Romans 1:26

2. **Homosexual lifestyle**....*And likewise also the men, leaving the natural use of the woman, burned in their lust one toward another; men with men working that which is unseemly, and receiving in themselves that recompence of their error which was meet.* Romans 1:27

3. **Refusal To Acknowledge God**...*And even as they did not like to retain God in their knowledge, God gave them over to a reprobate mind, to do those things which are not convenient;* Romans 1:28

4. **Unrighteous To The Bone**....*Being filled with all unrighteousness, fornication, wickedness, covetousness, maliciousness; full of envy, murder, debate, deceit, malignity; whisperers, backbiters, haters of God, despiteful, proud, boasters, inventors of evil things, disobedient to parents, without understanding, covenantbreakers, without natural affection, implacable, unmerciful* (In other words...Immoral) Romans 1:29-31

5. **Disobedient And Rebellious**...*Who knowing the judgment of God, that they which commit such things are worthy of death, not only do the same, but have pleasure in them that do them.* Romans 1:32

I think it's important to understand the meaning for some of the words used in #4 above. Most of us know what they mean but some are not used in today's expressions and may not be as familiar.

Fornication...is generally consensual sexual intercourse between two people not married to each other. ... For many people, the term carries an overtone of moral or religious disapproval. Throughout history, most theologians have argued that any and all forms of premarital sex are immoral. A contemporary example is the modern-day theologian Lee Gatiss who argues that premarital sex is immoral based on scripture. He states that, from a Biblical perspective, "physical union should not take place outside a "one flesh" (i.e. marriage) union.

Wickedness...*The state of being wicked; a mental disregard for justice, righteousness, truth, honor, virtue; evil in thought and life; depravity; sinfulness; criminality. See SIN. Many words are rendered "wickedness." There are many synonyms for wickedness in English and also in the Hebrew. Pride and vanity lead to it:*

Covetousness... Strong desire to have that, which belongs to another. It is considered to be a very grievous offense in Scripture. The tenth commandment forbids coveting anything that belongs to a neighbor, including his house, his wife, his servants, his ox or donkey, or anything that belongs to him (Exod 20:17). Jesus listed covetousness or greed along with many of the sins from within, including adultery, theft, and murder, which make a person unclean (Mr 7:22). Paul reminded the Ephesians that greed or covetousness is equated with immorality and impurity, so that these must be put away (5:3). A covetous or greedy person is an idolater (5:5) and covetousness is idolatry (Col 3:5). James warns that people kill and covet because they cannot have what they want (4:2).

Maliciousness...or Malice," now used in the sense of deliberate ill-will, by its derivation means badness, or wickedness generally, and was so used in Older English. In the Apocrypha it is the translation of kakia, "evil," "badness." We have "malice" in the more restricted sense as the translation of menis, "confirmed anger." In the New Testament "malice" and "maliciousness" are the translation of kakia (Romans 1:29; 1 Corinthians 5:8; 14:20; Colossians

3:8); malicious is the translation of poneros, "evil" (3John 1:10, malignity occurs in Romans 1:29 as the translation of kakoetheia, "evil disposition"; "maliciously," "having ill will."

Malignity... malice, malevolence, ill will, spite, **malignity**, spleen, grudge mean the desire to see another experience pain, injury, or distress. Malice implies a deep-seated often-unexplainable desire to see another suffer.

Despiteful... adjective. Characterized by intense ill will or spite: black, evil, hateful, malevolent, malicious, malign, malignant, mean, nasty, poisonous, spiteful, venomous, vicious, wicked. Slang: bitchy.

Without Natural Affection... This phrase "without natural affection" is the translation of one Greek word, *astergeo*. It was a characteristic of many pagans of the ancient world. Significantly, it is also prophesied to be a characteristic of the humanistic pagans of the end-times. "In the last days . . . men shall be . . . without natural affection" (II Timothy 3:1-3). These are the only two occurrences of this word in the New Testament.

The word *stergeo* ("natural affection") is one of four Greek words for "love," but it is never used at all in the New Testament. It refers to the natural love that members of the same family have for each other. It is such a common characteristic of all peoples that there was apparently no occasion to refer to it at all -- *except* when it is *not* present, when people lose their instinctive love for their own parents and children, and thus are "*without* natural affection." One thinks of the widespread abortions of these last days, as well as the modern breakdown of the family in general.

Implacable... not placable: not capable of being appeased, significantly changed, or mitigated and *implacable* enemy.

Let's Paint A Portrait

Some folks see only with their five senses. If they can't smell it, feel it, taste it or otherwise use their natural senses, it doesn't exist. However, there are those that see with their spirit and feel with their heart. They look at such things as character, morals, and commitment.

Those that see with the spirit paint a portrait of the damned with character that reveals itself in personality traits and actions. Jesus, referring to false prophets said, "Ye shall know them by their fruits." Matthew 7:16

Paul, the apostle, tells us about the fruit of the Spirit in his letter to the Galatians. He says, "But the fruit of the Spirit is love, peace, joy, patience, kindness, goodness, faithfulness, is <u>love</u>, <u>joy</u>, <u>peace</u>, <u>patience</u>, <u>kindness</u>, <u>goodness</u>, <u>faithfulness</u>, <u>gentleness</u> and self control. This fruit is in fact the very character of God.

The fruit is contrasted with the *works of the flesh*, which are also found in Galatians chapter five. They have already been discussed.

So, to see a person that has been damned by God, you will see a person that is a murderer; One who is caught up in habitual envying of others; one who allows hate to dwell in their heart, one that commits adultery against his or her spouse; one who is into sexual immorality; one who fights against peace to create strife; one who puts idols above God and worships them; one who participates in witchcraft (The worship of Devils);

These folks are soiled, <u>filthy</u>, <u>base</u>, <u>unchaste</u>, <u>sinful</u>, <u>corrupt</u> and <u>polluted</u>. However, Paul says that this portrait, at one time, was a picture of them. They were the monsters that ruled the world in sin. See it for yourself in Paul's letters to Titus and the Colossian church.

"For we ourselves also were sometimes foolish, disobedient,

deceived, serving divers lusts and pleasures, living in malice and envy, hateful, and hating one another." Titus 3:3

"And you, that were sometime alienated and enemies in your mind by wicked works, yet now hath he reconciled In the body of his flesh through death, to present you holy and unblameable and unreproveable in his sight:" Colossians 1:21-22

You'll remember that God created man in his own images and in his likeness. Man was, originally, created to manifest the very character or nature of God on the earth. But, with the disobedience of one man, Adam, sin entered into the human race and death came as a result of that sin…so says Paul in his letter to the Romans.

"Wherefore, as by one man sin entered into the world, and death by sin; and so death passed upon all men, for that all have sinned:" Romans 5:12

"And you hath he quickened, who were dead in trespasses and sins; Wherein in time past ye walked according to the course of this world, according to the prince of the power of the air, the spirit that now works in the children of disobedience: Among whom also we all had our conversation in times past in the lusts of our flesh, fulfilling the desires of the flesh and of the mind; and were by nature the children of wrath, even as others."

From Death Into Life

Here's what these scriptures tell us about ourselves:

1. We were just like everyone else, dead in our sins.
2. We walked according to the lifestyle of this world, following the call of immorality.
3. We were slaves to Satan who rules the souls that are living on planet earth but dead spiritually.

4. We were children of wrath and disobedient against the will of God.
5. We talked the talk and walked the walk as people of the flesh, not the Spirit.
6. We were enemies of God, serving divers lusts and pleasures, living in malice and envy, hateful, and hating one another.

Aren't you glad that I said, "Were?" Paul goes on to say that Jesus reconciled us to God by his own death, as a penalty for sin. He did all of this so he could present us holy and unblameable and unreproveable before the throne of God.

The true gospel message is that God lost his most prized possession, Mankind. He lost Adam to disobedience and self-will that actually led him to attempt to be his own god. That was the same sin that Lucifer, otherwise know as Satan, and the Devil commuted.

The difference between Lucifer's sin and Adam's was Adam was deceived into believing a lie. Here's what Jesus said that later became the divine solution. He tossed Lucifer out of heaven and into chains of darkness. God, through Jesus' death, resurrection and righteous life, restored man to his rightful place in God's kingdom. God's great Love for us was manifested in Jesus.

"For God so loved the world, that he gave his only begotten Son, that whosoever believeth in him should not perish, but have everlasting life." John 3:16

Why did God do such a thing? *"For God sent not his Son into the world to condemn the world; but that the world through him might be saved."* John 3:17

How can you and I be saved and escape the wrath of God that he will pour out upon the wicked?

" He that believeth on him is not condemned: but he that believeth not is condemned already, because he hath not believed in the name

of the only begotten Son of God. And this is the condemnation, that light is come into the world, and men loved darkness rather than light, because their deeds were evil." John 3:18-19

Aliens And Strangers

The Bible says we are now Aliens in this world.

The Word of God tells us that we are *aliens and strangers* in this world. This means that this world is NOT our home. We do not belong here. To understand this better let's use an example: let's say that you board a plane and land in a country foreign to you. You are alien and foreigner in that country. You don't understand the language of the people. You cannot read their newspapers. You turn on the TV but you soon have to turn it off as you do not understand anything. It is all foreign to you. You are an alien and a stranger.

If however, using the same example, you start speaking the language of the people, listen to their news, watch their TV programs, speak about what they speak and do what they do, you are no longer a stranger and an alien, but you are integrated to that country, you are part of it. It is the same for us as Christians.

The Word of God tells us that we are strangers and aliens to this world. We are not supposed to be conformed to this world, to share the same interests with the world, behave as the world behaves, watch what the world watches and have the same vision and interests as the world has. We are strangers and aliens here and we are not supposed to be integrated or conformed to this world (Romans 12:2) i.e. be shaped together with the world (that's what co-formed means). We are coming from another world, another home. Where is this home? Here are a couple of passages that answer this:

Philippians 3:20…"For our citizenship is in heaven, from which we also eagerly wait for the Savior, the Lord Jesus Christ,.."

Colossians 1:12-13…"He (God) has delivered us from the power of darkness and conveyed us into the kingdom of the Son of his love," The Journal of Biblical Accuracy

"The Soul That Sinneth, It Shall Die."

I know that some folks that read this will be upset. After all, who am I to say that the entire world, every person, is full of sin and headed towards eternal destruction? However, I did say it but I did not originate the idea. God sets the rules. He said it first, *"The soul who sinneth, it shall die."* Ezekiel 18:20 I just happen to believe it, especially when Jesus backs it up. Here's what He said.

"Enter ye in at the strait gate: for wide is the gate, and broad is the way, that leads to destruction, and many there be which go in thereat: Because strait is the gate, and narrow is the way, which leads unto life, and few there be that find it." Matthew 7:13-14

"Repent ye therefore, and be converted, that your sins may be blotted out, when the times of refreshing shall come from the presence of the Lord." Acts 3:19

Most of the world is on that broad road that leads to destruction. The gate is wide and easily seen. The only way to enter the narrow gate is to repent (turn from your wicked ways) and receive Jesus as your savior.

Wait A Minute…I am a decent person. I try to be good, go to church occasionally, work hard and love my family, so why is God angry with me?

The measurement for which salvation is given is Holiness. We must be continually Holy, without even one blemish…no disobedience! No sin! If we miss the mark, we miss it, even if it is just by a few inches. In other words, we can never reach God's level because he is holy and righteousness. We are not, no matter how good we seem to be in the eyes or the eyes of others.

Again Paul, in his letters to the church, makes this clear. He says…

"For all have sinned and fall short of the glory of God." ... Paul wrote in Romans 2:10, "It is written: none is righteous, no, not one; no one understands; no one seeks for God."

Think About it...if God had looked at the human race as fixable, he would have fixed it with new laws or some easier mark to attain. But he, instead, saw mankind as totally depraved and thus concluded that there was no fixing it. He knew that mankind could not or would not ever attain holiness on their own merits. (Remember, holiness is moral purity) So...He deemed it all as spiritually dead so he could save it all through life, the life of Jesus.

Where is good works? Where are man's efforts to attain moral purity? The best of the best is still short of the mark. Man is still a slave to sin. Only Jesus could redeem mankind. Listen as you read this next scripture. It will show the truth.

"For if, when we were enemies, we were reconciled to God by the death of his Son, much more, being reconciled, we shall be saved by his life." Romans 5:10

The death of Jesus on the cross, reconciled us unto God. However, our salvation comes by His life. Where we fail, time after time, he did not. He lived the life we were supposed to live and he dies the death we were supposed to die.

Salvation

"That if thou shalt confess with thy mouth the Lord Jesus, and shalt believe in thine heart that God hath raised him from the dead, thou shalt be saved. For with the heart man believeth unto righteousness; and with the mouth confession is made unto salvation." Romans 10:9-10

It's that simple. Tell yourself and everybody else that your have made Jesus Lord of your life and believe in your heart that God raised him from the dead…and you shall be saved. This puts you on the narrow path that leads unto eternal life.

I think I have done a fair job of painting a portrait of the damned. Little did I know when I started this study that I would see myself and every other believer from Adam to the end of time in the portrait. Thank God I can say, it was in the past and not now. Thank God that I responded to the call, repented and received Jesus as my personal savior. How about you?

It saddens me to know that the entire world will soon come face to face with the wrath of God. However, all peoples of the earth have the knowledge of the one true and living God and they are all subject to his judgments. I am glad that I have found grace in his sight and will not suffer the terror of his wrath.

CHAPTER SIX

THE ANTI-CHRIST

HOPE THAT YOU NEVER RUN into "The Anti-Christ." He is the personification of evil in the flesh. He is the devil incarnate. If you fall under his rule, you will have missed the rapture of the church and will be in danger of hell fire.

Anti-Christ is an agenda that is gaining strength in our society and around the world. It is designed to rid the world of true followers of Jesus and all believers in the Most High God. Anyone that stands against the teaching of Jesus is considered to be an Anti-Christ. That would be billions in our world today. However, there will come a day when one man will rise up as the supreme leader of all the Anti-God folks to be the Anti-Christ.

The Bible teaches that just after the 2nd coming of Jesus Christ, when he returns to earth for his church, there will be a dynamic political leader that will arise on the world scene. This political leader will be a Satan possessed individual. He will quickly gain authority over all nations and peoples. It is assumed this authority will be given to him, without conflict, because he will have the answers to many of the world's problems. Revelation 13:7 He is known as, "The Anti-Christ"

The term "Anti-Christ" means just what it says, Anti or against Christ. Maybe you didn't know that Jesus' last name is not Christ. Christ is actually a Greek translation meaning, "Anointed." This is

New Testament. The Old Testament translation for "Anointed" is Messiah.

There are many deceivers in the world today but one day, "The Anti-Christ" will appear. *"For many deceivers are entered into the world, who confess not that Jesus Christ is come in the flesh. This is a deceiver and an Anti-Christ.* 2 John 1:7

Born Again believers are anointed by the Holy Sprit and can successfully stand against anyone that has an anti-Christ agenda. However, "The Anti-Christ" will be different. He will show miracles and lying wonders and deceive many. *"Even him*, whose coming is after the working of Satan with all power and signs and lying wonders" II Thessalonians 2:9

His arrival date is not known but we can discern the times. The Bible tells us that the Anti-Christ is being held back from appearing until God's children are safely out of harms way. This would be after the rapture of the church.

This is pictured in The Noah & The Ark story. His family was safely in the ark with the doors shut before the rains came. There was also Lot. He and his wife were safely led out of the city by angels before fire and brimstone fell from heaven. However, Christians still debate when Christ will return and when the Anti-Christ will appear.

The Rapture Controversy

There has always been a controversy over when Jesus will return to earth. Some say before the Anti-Christ is revealed or Pre-Tribulation. Others say not until the very end, after the tribulation period, or Post Tribulation. Then there is another crowd of folks that support a mid-tribulation event.

I hold to the Pre-Trib viewpoint. Here's why:

1. God's children will be spared from the wrath to come…The

Great Tribulation, that 7-year period when Satan indwells human flesh and becomes the Anti-Christ, is where God pours out His wrath on the wicked. *"And to wait for his Son from heaven, whom he raised from the dead, even Jesus, which delivered us from the wrath to come."* I Thessalonians 1:10

The scripture is clear that the, "wrath to come", is not directed towards God's children. Jesus delivered us from that by dying for our sins and because we have put our trust in Him.

2. The Anti-Christ cannot be revealed until the Holy Spirit is taken out of the way. Hear the words of Paul: II Thessalonians 2:3-10

"Let no man deceive you by any means: for *that day shall not come*, except there come a falling away first, and that man of sin be revealed, the son of perdition; Who opposeth and exalteth himself above all that is called God, or that is worshipped; so that he as God sitteth in the temple of God, shewing himself that he is God. Remember ye not, that, when I was yet with you, I told you these things?

And now ye know what withholdeth that he might be revealed in his time. For the mystery of iniquity doth already work: only he who now letteth (Restrains) *will let (Restrain)*, <u>until he be taken out of the way</u>. And then shall that Wicked be revealed, whom the Lord shall consume with the spirit of his mouth, and shall destroy with the brightness of his coming: *Even him*, whose coming is after the working of Satan with all power and signs and lying wonders, And with all deceivableness of unrighteousness in them that perish; because they received not the love of the truth, that they might be saved."

Note: The "He That Letteth" is the Holy Spirit. He is restraining or holding back the full manifestation of evil in human flesh. He will continue to do so until he is taken out of the way." II Thessalonians 2:7

You'll remember what Jesus said, *"I will not leave you comfortless: I will come to you."* John 14:18 *"But the Comforter, which is the Holy Ghost, whom the Father will send in my name, he shall teach you all things, and bring all things to your remembrance, whatsoever I have said unto you."* John 14:26

The comforter is the Holy Spirit and he lives in us. 1st Corinthians 3:16 says... *"Know ye not that ye are the temple of God, and that the Spirit of God dwells in you?"* When he goes, we will go with him. Otherwise, Jesus would be breaking his word and backing out of a promise. He will not do that.

3. The Post-Tribulation theory goes against what Jesus said to His disciples. "But of that day and that hour knoweth no man, no, not the angels which are in heaven, neither the Son, but the Father. *"Take ye heed, watch and pray: for ye know not when the time is."* Mark 13:32-37,

The most important characteristic of Christ's return is that it could happen without warning, suddenly, catching us off guard.

If the post tribulation theories were correct then we would know absolutely that Christ couldn't return until after the Rapture (which would make Matthew 24:42-44 impossible). How can we watch for the Lord's imminent and sudden return if he cannot return until after all the tragic events of the 7-year tribulation period (as taught in the book of Revelation)?

The only logical and workable conclusion is Pre-Tribulation Rapture, that is, the Rapture will take place before the tribulation period. Excerpts from article by David Stewart www.jesusissavor.com

The Origin of The Anti-Christ

Many folks believe that the Anti-Christ will come out of the Jewish nation. However this theory has some major problems, one being, the Jews will reject him as their Messiah when he proclaims himself to be God. If he was Jewish and performs lying wonders and miracles, they would most likely accept him as their messiah, but they do not.

Daniel 9:26 tells us that he will either rise out of the old Roman Empire or his lineage will be that from the area of the old Roman Empire. The "Prince that shall come" will come out of "The people" who "shall destroy the city". Since it was Rome and its legions that destroyed Jerusalem in AD 70, it logically follows that the "prince that shall come" must come out of the Roman Empire and people.

The Jews will accept the Anti-Christ as a political leader that will save the day as to war and other problems.

He will be a gentile, not a Jew. The Bible tells us that the Anti-Christ will arise out of "the sea" (Daniel 7:2-3, Revelation 132:1) indicating that he will arise out of the gentile nations, not Israel.

His origin doesn't really matter. All that matters is that we know he is a real person full of satanic powers and evil. One day, we will see him as he really is and say, *" Is this the man that made the earth to tremble, that did shake kingdoms"* Isaiah 14:16

The # 666
Mark of The Beast

The number 666 is most often associated with the beast of revelation 13:17-18. It is what is called, *"The Mark of The Beast."* The Beast is the anti-Christ and his mark is 666, the number of man. In modern popular culture, 666 has become one of the most widely recognized symbols for the Anti-Christ or, alternatively, the devil. The number 666 is purportedly used to invoke Satan.

The number 666 is based on a Hebrew system of numerology called "Gematria" and refers to the sinfulness of man, as well as the rise of the "Beast," or Satan, as Jesus Christ prepares to return to earth. It is mentioned in the last book of the New Testament, "Revelation."

"Here is wisdom. Let him that hath understanding count the number of the beast: for it is the number of a man; and his number is Six hundred threescore and six." Revelation 13:18

This number is the mark of the beast. It will play a large part during the 7-years of the great tribulation. People will not be able to buy or sell anything unless they have this mark. It will be on their forhead or in the palm of their hand. Some have speculated that the mark of the beast will be a type of chip or simular to a credit card.

The Anti-Christ As A Person

Even though the Bible does not tell us exactly who the Anti-Christ is, the scriptures are very clear on what traits and characteristics he will possess, when he will come onto the world stage, and what he will do once he takes power.

He will be appealing, not repulsive. The Bible refers to the Anti-Christ as a blasphemous horn (Daniel 7:25-25), as lawless (2 Thessalonians 2:3-4), and a beast (Revelation 13:1-2) hardly an attractive list of descriptions, but we know that people will follow him (Revelation 13:3), so he will present himself as an alluring leader – at first. He will be super, not ordinary; everything about the Anti-Christ will be extraordinary. He will possess great eloquence, charm, wit, military genius, vision, and intelligence. He will be extremely influential, charismatic, a false champion of peace, and will possess strong leadership abilities. One could even say he's a rock star.

Daniel 8:23-24 tells us that the Anti-Christ is a king with fierce countenance, and understanding dark sentences, which means he will be deeply involved with occult mysteries. He will be filled with satanic power (and later become possessed by Satan). (Excerpts from David Jeremiah of www.arewelivinginthelastdays.com.

Early Christians tended to emphasize the coming of the one great Anti-Christ. The Revelation to John refers to this figure as "The Beast from the Abyss" (11:7) and "the Beast from the Sea" (13:1). In the most sustained account of his appearance, II Thessalonians 2:1-12, he is called "the man of sin" and "son of perdition." He will come at a time of a general apostasy, deceive people with signs and wonders, sit in the temple of God, and claim to be God himself. Finally, he will be defeated by Jesus, who will destroy him by "the spirit of his mouth" and "the brightness of his coming" (2:8). *Robert E. Lerner*

Most Bible prophecy experts believe the Anti-Christ will be the ultimate embodiment of what it means to be against Christ. In the end times/last hour, a man will arise to oppose Christ and his followers more than anyone else in history. Likely claiming to be the true Messiah, the Anti-Christ will seek world domination and will attempt to destroy all followers of Jesus Christ that were saved after the rapture and the nation of Israel.

Other Names For The Anti-Christ

Throughout the Bible, the Anti-Christ bears many titles: Son of Perdition, Man of Sin, Man of Lawlessness, Prince of Destruction, Abomination, and the Beast.

The prophet Daniel describes the man in great detail: He shall be an evil king who will "…exalt himself and magnify himself above every god and shall speak outrageous things against the God of gods, and shall prosper until the indignation is accomplished: for that which has been determined shall come to pass.

Neither shall he regard the God of his fathers, nor the desire of women, nor regard any god: for he shall magnify himself above all. But in his estate he shall (secretly) honor a god of forces and a god whom his fathers never knew. To these he will worship with gold and silver and with precious stones and pleasant things. Thus shall he do in his fortress with a strange god, whom he shall acknowledge and increase with glory; and he shall cause them to rule over many and shall divide the land for gain" (Daniel 11:36).

Thoughts of Three Noted Scholars

Dr. Ed Hinson....While there is no clear prophecy about the United States of America in the Bible (nor Canada, Australia, South Africa, and so on), it is certainly probable that if a European alliance were to form in fulfillment of these prophecies anytime soon, it would most likely include all the major Western powers. That they could be headed by an American leader is certainly possible, even probable."

Charles Swindoll....While Daniel pondered the vision of the ten future kings (Nebuchadnezzar's dream) (Daniel 7:8), he saw something new, that a "little horn" (an eleventh king, a man) will rise up among the nations of the original ten kings. The "little horn" (the Anti-Christ) will subdue three of the ten kings and destroy their political power. The seven surviving kings of the original 10 nations will submit to the domination of the "little horn". This earthly leader will then begin his role as Anti-Christ and world dictator.

Hal Lindsey... Notice in Daniel's description in Daniel 7:8 "and three of the first horns were uprooted before it". This could either be referring to a bloody conflict that will destroy three nations or regions of this confederacy that opposes the Anti-Christ's taking over of power but more likely it is referring to the removal (assassination) of the leaders of three regions in this confederacy who opposes the Anti-Christ's taking over the confederacy (global government).

Anti-Christ
The Man of Your Choice

Over the years, the folks that study the Bible have tried to pin the name," Anti-Christ", on a popular leader or figure. Hitler was one. Kennedy was another. The list goes on and on. Most recent is the catholic Pope. It would not be the 1st time. Martin Luther pinned the Pope of his day when he initiated the protestant reformation.

Pastor Robert James Jeffers, Jr., of the First Baptist Church of Dallas, Texas told Christianity Today magazine that although President Obama was certainly not the Anti-Christ, his policies paved the way for the Anti-Christ. He said, "While I am not suggesting that President Obama is the Anti-Christ, the fact that he was able to propose such a sweeping change in God's law and still win re-election by a comfortable margin illustrates how a future world leader will be able to oppose God's laws without any repercussions."

Some of the objectionable perceived Anti-Christian policies Obama pushed include same-sex marriage and homosexual rights, as well as funding for Planned Parenthood and abortion in his signature Obamacare, the newspaper said.

New World Order

For the United Nations Interfaith movement, and many new age, ecumenical groups, there is a rising expectation of a universal messiah. The Lucis Trust, once called the Lucifer Foundation, has heavily influenced the United Nations from its founding. At its roots are occult secret societies such as Freemasons, Wicca, and the Order of the Golden Dawn. Robert Muller and Maurice Strong, influential in the founding of the United Nations, are adept new age advocates who tirelessly promote the blending of all religious faiths.

The "Son of Perdition"

Advocates of the New World Order will attempt to fulfill the world's messianic expectations with one man. We Christians call him the Anti-Christ.

2 Thessalonians 2:3-4 tells us that the *Day of Christ*, where he sets up his kingdom, will not come until "the man of sin is revealed, the son of perdition," commonly called the Anti-Christ.

He will sit in the temple in Jerusalem and demand to be worshipped as God. This tyrannical world dictator empowered by Satan and the embodiment of all that is opposed to God. Christ at his Second Coming will defeat him. (II Thessalonians 2:8).

War With The Saints

Daniel 7:21,25 tells us that the Anti-Christ will make war with the saints. Some use this as an objection to a pre-tribulation rapture. If the saints are gone in the rapture, how can they still be on earth fighting with the Anti-Christ?

The answer is easy. You just need to know who are the 144,000. "Then I heard the number of those who were sealed: 144,000 from all the tribes of Israel" (Revelation 7:4), nothing in the passage leads to interpreting the 144,000 as anything but a literal number of Jews—12,000 taken from every tribe of the "Sons of Israel." The New Testament offers no clear-cut text replacing Israel with the church.

These Jews are "sealed," which means they have the special protection of God from all of the divine judgments and from the Anti-Christ to perform their mission during the tribulation period (see

Revelation 6:17, in which people will wonder who can stand from the wrath to come).

The tribulation period is a future seven-year period of time in which God will enact divine judgment against those who reject him and will complete his plan of salvation for the nation of Israel. All of this is according to God's revelation to the prophet Daniel (Daniel 9:24–27).

The 144,000 Jews are a sort of "first fruits" (Revelation 14:4) of a redeemed Israel, which were previously prophesied (Zechariah 12:10; Romans 11:25–27), and their mission seems to be to evangelize the post-rapture world and proclaim the gospel during the tribulation period. As a result of their ministry, millions—"a great multitude that no one could number, from every nation, tribe, people and language" (Revelation 7:9)—will come to faith in Christ. These are those that the Anti-Christ makes war with.

So, the saints that war with the Anti-Christ are Jews and their converts that go through the great tribulation.

The Battle of Armageddon

This frightening apocalyptic word "Armageddon" refers to earth's final battle which is generally referred to as the Battle of Armageddon. But who are the contestants of this great battle of Armageddon? A fairly common reply would be "Russia, Syria, or Iran against Israel." As the Middle East simmers toward a boiling point, and as U.S., British, and Israeli intelligence monitor closely Iran's quest for a nuclear bomb which might even be used against America, millions of Christians, Jews, Muslims, and even secularists are pondering, "Is the Battle of Armageddon at hand?" I believe so. Yet I am also convinced that there are massive battle of Armageddon illusions rampant everywhere. Please allow me to explain.

The word "Armageddon" appears only once in the entire Bible and is found in Revelation 16:16. If you open God's Word and read this passage yourself along with the verses immediately before and after it, you will be amazed at what you will find and not find in regards to the battle of Armageddon. Take a look for yourself: "And he gathered them together into a place called in the Hebrew tongue Armageddon." Rev. 16:16

Interestingly, no place on earth actually bears the name Armageddon, and the above passage is the only mention of it in scripture and hence it is assumed that this is what scripture refers to but is it? The Greek is most commonly thought to be a transliteration of the Hebrew *har megiddo*, literally, "mountain of Megiddo."

The Mount of Megiddo is located in the plain of Esdraelon or Jezreel, a valley fourteen by twenty miles in size located to the southwest of Nazareth. Here, it is thought by many, that the great final battle of Armageddon will be fought at the end of time.

The Anti-Christ's Destiny

It should be obvious by now that the destiny of this "Evil One" is not good. Here's what the scripture says…

Revelation 19:20: "And the beast was taken, and with him the false prophet that wrought miracles before him, with which he deceived them that had received the mark of the beast, and them that worshipped his image. These both were cast alive into a lake of fire burning with brimstone. "

Revelation 20:10: "And the devil that deceived them was cast into the lake of fire and brimstone, where the beast and the false prophet are, and shall be tormented day and night for ever and ever."

In summary, the Anti-Christ is the end-times false messiah who seeks, and likely achieves, world domination so that he can destroy Israel and all followers of Jesus Christ.

His efforts, although powerfully evil, fail. Millions still come to a saving knowledge of Jesus, the Christ of God. Many are martyred for their faith and still millions will survive the ordeal to see Jesus set up his kingdom on earth. These are they that are spoken of by Jesus in Matthew 25. *"Then the King will say to those on His right, 'Come, you who are blessed of My Father, inherit the kingdom prepared for you from the foundation of the world"* Matthew 25:34.

The wrath of God will fall on the wicked and the battle of the ages will be over. Jesus will have gathered all to himself who wanted to be with God and dwell with him for eternity.

The best news of all is, we who are "Born Again", will not experience the wrath of God that is to come. We will be raptured (caught up together in the air) to be with Jesus. Then we will return with him, riding on heavenly horses back to earth to establish his kingdom.

If you are not, "Born Again" read John 3:16 and do what Jesus tells you. You don't want to be left behind to face the onslaught of evil at its worst. God loves you and wants to keep you from experiencing his wrath.

CHAPTER SEVEN

BATTLE OF THE AGES

THE GREATEST BATTLE OF ALL times is the battle for the souls of mankind. It is a life and death struggle for every human being. It crosses ethnic groups, geographical boarders, social status, and all other lines that segment people into different levels. No one is exempt. We are all targets for the enemy of God.

If you think this is not true, read I Peter 5:8-9 "Be sober, be vigilant; because your adversary the devil, as a roaring lion, walks about, seeking whom he may devour: Whom resist stedfast in the faith, knowing that the same afflictions are accomplished in your brethren that are in the world."

This chapter is designed to expose our enemy and his tricks so we do not fall prey to his dominance and subsequent control. We will be looking at God's original plan for man and how Satan destroyed it. We will also be looking at God's provision for man after he lost his way.

God wants us to fight the good fight of faith all the way to the end of the age. He wants us to stay free and live in good health and rule over our world until he comes back. The end of the world is at hand but that does not mean we are to be slack or give up on what is true and right. Our job, as believers, is not to fall asleep at the wheel but to stand and declare the goodness and love of God, our heavenly Father.

The Enemy of Our Souls

Peter describes our enemy as, *"your adversary the devil"* as he writes his second letter to various churches in Asia Minor sometime between 64 AD and 68 AD. He does not say Nero or the Romans in general are their enemy. Instead, he points his finger directly at the devil and tells them that this evil intenty is their adversary.

An adversary, according to the dictionary is, "a person, group, or force that opposes or attacks; opponent; enemy; foe."

The Bible calls Satan by many different names, including the devil, but he is still the same sinister opponent that we have to face in battle every waking moment. Here's a list for your review:

Accuser

"Then I heard a loud voice saying in heaven, 'Now salvation, and strength, and the kingdom of our God, and the power of His Christ have come, for the *accuser of our brethren*, who accused them before our God day and night, has been cast down.'" Revelation 12:10

Adversary

"Be sober, be vigilant; because your adversary the devil walks about like a roaring lion, seeking whom he may devour." 1 Peter 5:8

Angel of light

"And no wonder! For Satan himself transforms himself into an angel of light." II Corinthians 11:14

Anti-Christ

"And every spirit that does not confess that Jesus Christ has come in the flesh is not of God. And this is the spirit of the Anti-Christ, which you have heard was coming, and is now already in the world." 1 John 4:3

Beelzebub

"Now when the Pharisees heard it they said, 'this fellow does not cast out demons except by Beelzebub, the ruler of the demons.*"* Matthew 12:24

Belial

"And what accord has Christ with Belial? Or what part has a believer with an unbeliever?" II Corinthians 6:15

Deceiver

"So the great dragon was cast out, that serpent of old, called the devil and Satan, who deceives the whole world; he was cast to the earth, and his angels were cast out with him." Revelation 12:9

Devil

"He who sins is of the devil, for the devil has sinned from the beginning. For this purpose the Son of God was manifested, that He might destroy the works of the devil." 1 John 3:8

Dragon

"So the great dragon was cast out, that serpent of old, called the devil and Satan, who deceives the whole world; he was cast to the earth, and his angels were cast out with him." Revelation 12:9

Enemy

"The enemy who sowed them is the devil, the harvest is the end of the age, and the reapers are the angels." Matthew 13:39

Evil One

"I do not pray that you should take them out of the world, but that you should keep them from the evil one." John 17:15

Father of Lies

"You are of your father the devil, and the desires of your father you want to do. He was a murderer from the beginning, and does not stand in the truth, because there is no truth in him. When he speaks a lie, he speaks from his own resources, for he is a liar and the father of it." John 8:44

God of This World

"Whose minds the god of this world has blinded, who do not believe, lest the light of the gospel of the glory of Christ, who is the image of God, should shine on them." 2 Corinthians 4:4

Lawless One

"And then the lawless one will be revealed, whom the Lord will consume with the breath of His mouth and destroy with the brightness of his coming. The coming of the lawless one is according to the working of Satan, with all power, signs, and lying wonders, and with all unrighteous deception among those who perish, because they did not receive the love of the truth, that they might be saved." II Thessalonians 2:8-10

Leviathan

"In that day the LORD with his severe sword, great and strong, Will punish Leviathan the fleeing serpent, Leviathan that twisted serpent; And He will slay the reptile that is in the sea." Isaiah 27:1

Liar

"You are of your father the devil, and the desires of your father you want to do. He was a murderer from the beginning, and does not stand in the truth, because there is no truth in him. When he speaks a lie, he speaks from his own resources, for he is a liar and the father of it." John 8:44

Lucifer

"How you are fallen from heaven, O Lucifer, son of the morning!

How you are cut down to the ground? You who weakened the nations!

For you have said in your heart: 'I will ascend into heaven, I will exalt my throne above the stars of God; I will also sit on the mount of the congregation on the farthest sides of the north; I will ascend above the heights of the clouds, I will be like the Most High." Isaiah 14:12-14

Man of Sin

"Let no one deceive you by any means; for that Day will not come unless the falling away comes first, and the man of sin is revealed, the son of perdition, who opposes and exalts himself above all that is called God or that is worshiped, so that he sits as God in the temple of God, showing himself that he is God." 2 Thessalonians 2:3,4

Murderer

"You are of your father the devil, and the desires of your father you want to do. He was a murderer from the beginning, and does not stand in the truth, because there is no truth in him. When he speaks a lie, he speaks from his own resources, for he is a liar and the father of it." John 8:44

Prince of The Power of The Air

"And you He made alive, who were dead in trespasses and sins, in which you once walked according to the course of this world, according to the prince of the power of the air, the spirit who now works in the sons of disobedience." Ephesians 2:1,2

Roaring Lion

"Be sober, be vigilant; because your adversary the devil walks about like a roaring lion, seeking whom he may devour." 1 Peter 5:8

Rulers of The Darkness

"For we do not wrestle against flesh and blood, but against principalities, against powers, against the rulers of the darkness of this age, against spiritual hosts of wickedness in the heavenly places." Ephesians 6:12

Prince of This World

"Now is the judgment of this world; now the prince of this world will be cast out. And I, if I am lifted up from the earth, will draw all peoples to me." John 12:31,32

Satan

"And He was there in the wilderness forty days, tempted by Satan, and was with the wild beasts; and the angels ministered to him." Mark 1:13

Serpent of Old

"So the great dragon was cast out, that serpent of old, called the devil and Satan, who deceives the whole world; he was cast to the earth, and his angels were cast out with him." Revelation 12:9

Son of Perdition

" Let no one deceive you by any means; for that day will not come unless the falling away comes first, and the man of sin is revealed, the son of perdition, who opposes and exalts himself above all that is called God or that is worshiped, so that he sits as God in the temple of God, showing himself that he is God." 2 Thessalonians 2:3,4

Tempter

"Now when the tempter came to him, he said, 'If you are the Son of God, command that these stones become bread." Matthew 4:3

Thief

"The thief does not come except to steal, and to kill, and to destroy. I have come that they may have life, and that they may have it more abundantly." John 10:10

Wicked One

"Above all, taking the shield of faith with which you will be able to quench all the fiery darts of the wicked one." Ephesians 6:16

This list of names for Satan has been taken from the New King James Version of the Bible.

There may be other names for Satan in the Bible. This is a partial list on the Internet developed by Nora Roth, a bible student. I offer her list because it is very accurate.

It should be evident by now, from all the names, that our enemy is bent on killing us or at best, keeping us from learning the truth about God and his love. These names form a portrait of evil. However, they also reveal how Satan operates.

It's like we have been given the playbook of the opposing team so we can learn their plays and develop a defense against them.

Here's what I see:

1. We will have to deal with lies that are made against us.
2. We will be accused day and night by evil forces that watch our every move.
3. We will be tempted with stuff that appeals to our own lust and fallen nature.
4. We will be fighting deception on every hand
5. We will see the truth becomes a lie and the lie accepted as truth in our society.
6. We will have to guard our hearts and protect our stuff against a masterful thief that stalks us daily.
7. We will have to exercise a lot of faith to keep from being hurt by "fiery darts" being hurled by the Wicked One.
8. We will have to wrestle against principalities, against powers, against the rulers of the darkness of this age, against spiritual hosts of wickedness in the heavenly places who are bent on our destruction.

The Devil's Crowd

It is true that our battle is with demons who are spiritual beings bent on our destruction. However, the devil also works through people. I call them, "The Devil's Crowd" This group consists of folks that deny Jesus as coming in the flesh. They are those that the Bible calls, "Anti-Christs". They support abortion, same sex marriage, child pornography, wife swapping, and all the liberal agenda currently being pushed in our society.

Sadly enough, these folks are in many instances, our parents, kids, neighbors, political officials and co-workers. Satan uses them to spread his Anti-Christ message.

My wife, just for the fun of it, searched the Internet for crime in our area. She found all sorts of evil going on, all within one mile from our home. Now that's scary. However, Satan will use anyone that is not on guard spiritually to attack God's children. He has a host of demons that do his bidding and they are relentless. However, Jesus defeated all the powers of darkness and gave us his victory. In his name, we can overcome the wiles of the devil.

The Battle Leading Up To The End

The battleground, where all the fighting takes place, is in your mind. You may be on a playground, at work, with family or friends but victory or defeat is all about how you think. Listen to what Paul told the early church.

"And be not conformed to this world: but be ye transformed by the renewing of your mind, that ye may prove what is that good, and acceptable, and perfect, will of God." Romans 12:2

Here the voices of the Old Testament Prophets

"And all this assembly shall know that the Lord saves not with sword and spear: *for the battle is the Lord's, and he will give you into our hands.*" 1st Samuel 17:47

"And it shall be, when thou shalt hear a sound of going in the tops of the mulberry trees, that then thou shalt go out to battle: *for God is gone forth before thee* to smite the host of the Philistines." I Chronicles 14:15

"Who is this King of glory? The Lord strong and mighty, *the Lord mighty in battle.*" Psalm 24:8

"Therefore he hath poured upon him the fury of his anger, and the strength of battle: and it hath set him on fire round about, yet he

knew not; and it burned him, yet he laid it not to heart." Isaiah 42:25

"Thou art my battle axe and weapons of war: for with thee will I break in pieces the nations, and with thee will I destroy kingdoms;" Jeremiah 51:20

There is some good news so don't get too depressed. I've said this before but it is worth repeating.

First, *The battle is the Lords*. " Thus saith the Lord unto you, be not afraid nor dismayed by reason of this great multitude; for the battle is not yours, but God's." II Chronicles 20:15 God wants us to know that he has everything under control.

Secondly, *God has given us his amour to wear so we don't get hurt*. "Finally, my brethren, be strong in the Lord, and in the power of his might. Put on the whole armor of God, that ye may be able to stand against the wiles of the devil. For we wrestle not against flesh and blood, but against principalities, against powers, against the rulers of the darkness of this world, against spiritual wickedness in high places. ...Ephesians 6:10-18

Thirdly, *Jesus has already defeated every evil power*. "And having despoiled principalities and powers, he made a show of them openly, triumphing over them in it." Colossians 2:15

The victory was at the cross where he died as a sacrifice for sin. "For what the law could not do, in that it was weak through the flesh, God sending his own Son in the likeness of sinful flesh, and for sin, condemned sin in the flesh:" Romans 8:3

Finally, *God wants us to walk in the Spirit so we do not fulfill the deeds of the flesh*. "This I say then, Walk in the Spirit, and ye shall not fulfill the lust of the flesh." Galatians 5:16 The deeds of the flesh are listed in Galatians 5. It is the flesh that causes us all the problems.

Paul tells us in Romans 8 that living in the flesh is to be carnally minded and that cannot be blessed of God or favored in any way. It brings only death to our souls. God is in the business of bringing life not death to our souls.

A sobering thought…this evil nature that is seen in Satan, who is our mortal enemy, has somehow manifested his nature in us. The deeds of the flesh are identical to the personality of the devil. How can this be? God did not create us this way.

The Creation of Man, His Fall And Restoration
Genesis 1:26-28

"And God said, Let us make man in our image, after our likeness: and let them have dominion over the fish of the sea, and over the fowl of the air, and over the cattle, and over all the earth, and over every creeping thing that creeps upon the earth. So God created man in his own image, in the image of God created he him; male and female created he them. And God blessed them, and God said unto them, Be fruitful, and multiply, and replenish the earth, and subdue it: and have dominion over the fish of the sea, and over the fowl of the air, and over every living thing that moves upon the earth." Genesis 1:26-28

Note: God created man in His image and likeness. What do we know about the likeness and image of God? Only this…it is a holy image and a righteous likeness. (Galatians 5:22) There is no sin in him. Yet man is all of a sudden filled with another image…that of Satan. Paul tells us all about what really happened to Adam and how it affected our destiny.

"Wherefore, as by one man sin entered into the world, and death by sin; and so death passed upon all men, for that all have sinned:" Romans 5:12

Adam was a prototype, the 1st of many to come. However, with his disobedience came sin instead of holiness. Instead of righteousness flowing from Adam to his descendants, sin overtook them all. Instead of the image of God remaining in Adam and being duplicated in his descendants, the nature and character of Satan filled the souls of man. Paul refers to Christ as the 2nd Adam. "And so it is written, the first man, Adam, was made a living soul; the last Adam *was made* a quickening spirit." I Corinthians 15:45

Some will disagree with me about Adam falling from God's grace and creating a world of sin. They will say that we are all children of God. However Romans 8:14 tells us, "For as many as are led by the Spirit of God, they are the sons of God.

There is another logical argument for the fall of man. It is in Genesis. It would be wrong to say that God created man in his own image, verse 1:26, and that image was both good and evil. To say such a thing is to say that God is also the devil, which is ludicrous. God is pure and morally righteous. He does not change. There is no darkness in him. That means that man had to change. He chose to disobey God and lost his innocence. Instead of God's image, he accepted the image of Satan. In this context, image equals character.

Here's how that all happened, according to the bible. It's recorder in Genesis chapter three, "Now the serpent was more crafty than any of the wild animals the Lord God had made. He said to the woman, "Did God really say, 'You must not eat from any tree in the garden'?" The woman said to the serpent, "We may eat fruit from the trees in the garden, but God did say, 'You must not eat fruit from the tree that is in the middle of the garden, and you must not touch it, or you will die." "You will not certainly die," the serpent said to the woman. "For God knows that when you eat from it your eyes will be opened, and you will be like God, knowing good and evil."

Note: the lie that Satan tells Eve is three-fold

1. "You will not surely die"
2. "You will be like God"
3. "You will know good and evil"

They were already like God, in that…they bore His image and likeness. They were not supposed to know evil. It was not in God's plan for man. What really happened was they knew evil by nature but lost the ability to know good.

Death was swift and sure but not physical, only spiritual. Physical came later. The Spirit's breath put into Adam was taken away and therefore it could not pass on to his descendants. That's why the New Testament says we must be, "Born Again".

Satan always tells lies to deceive us. If we buy the lie, we live out that destiny. If, on the other hand, we know the truth, it will set us free to shape our own destiny in accordance with God's will.

Knowing the truth is the greatest weapon we can have and use against evil influences. If you are not sure of what is truth, read the Bible. It is full of God's Word. Here's an example of how to use it to defeat Satan.

The enemy says to you, in the form of a thought that pops into your head, "You can rob a store and get the needed cash to buy that thing you've always wanted" "If no one sees you, you're Scott Free" "That company is insured anyway and will not miss what you steal" A simple declaration of truth will dispel the lies and keep your mind in focus with God's Will. Here's the declaration, *"Thou Shalt not Steal"* The truth of God's Word will always dispel the lie and expose its source.

So Adam fell from God's grace when he disobeyed God's command. His transgression was so bad that God could not fix it without violating man's free will to choose his own destiny. Adam chose to experience evil and he did...and so did we. However, there's always a, "But God" in every divine story.

Man Is Restored By God

But God didn't leave Adam and Eve to a hell-bound destiny. He, from before the foundation of the world, had a plan to redeem his greatest creation. The apostle John records Jesus as he tells Nicodemus, a religious leader, the plan of redemption. John 3:16 "For God so loved the world, that he gave his only begotten Son, that whosoever believeth in him should not perish, but have everlasting life."

It's important to note that salvation is available/given to every, "Whosoever" that believes. All that is necessary is to believe that God sent Jesus, his only Son to redeem mankind. Jesus is the only way to God and that is through the, "Born Again" experience.

Just "One Way To God?"
True or False?

It is hard for most folks that are not "Born Again" to understand why there is just one way to God, yet it is true. There is only one way and that is through Jesus Christ. The Bible is our source to prove that the one-way doctrine is valid. Acts 4:12 says, "Neither is there salvation in any other: for there is none other name under heaven given among men, whereby we must be saved."

Jesus is the only way to attain salvation. All the world religions cannot save us. Joining a church or specific faith cannot save us. It must be an acknowledgment of our sin, our cry before the throne of God for forgiveness, and our invitation for Jesus to come into our hearts and save us. His name is the only one that can get us through death into eternal life.

Here are a few scriptures that support the only "One-Way" doctrine.

1. ...There is one God, and one mediator between God and men, the man Christ Jesus; Who gave himself a ransom for all, to be testified in due time. (I Timothy 2:5-6)
2. ...Believe on the Lord Jesus Christ and thou shalt be saved... (Acts 16:31)
3. That if thou shalt confess with thy mouth the Lord Jesus, and shalt believe in thine heart that God hath raised him from the dead, THOU SHALT BE SAVED. For with the heart man believeth unto righteousness; and with the mouth confession is made unto salvation. (Romans 10:9-10)

The skeptic would say, "You mean to tell me that all the religions of the world are wrong and only Christianity is the one true religion?" Remember, Christianity is not a religion. It is a relationship born out of love between man and the one true and living God. There is no one true religion. Religion, in itself, will not get us to God. It is the blood of Christ that unlocks the door and our confession of faith in Jesus that makes it all happen. (John 14:6)

Why is Jesus the only way to God? ...Because God planned it that way. He set the penalty for sin, which was death. *The soul that sinneth, it shall die.* (Ezekiel 18:20) In fact, Jesus was the slain Lamb of God before the foundation of the world. (Ephesians 1:3-7)

Jesus himself said, as recorded in John 14:6, "I am the way, the truth, and the life: No man cometh to the Father but by me". Christianity states that the God of the Bible is the only true God and salvation is only possible by accepting Jesus Christ, his only begotten Son as Savior and Lord. II Corinthians 5:21 says, "For he hath made him to be sin for us, who knew no sin; that we might be made the righteousness of God in him."

God validated his Son as the only way in multiple ways so we could be assured that Jesus was indeed the only way to him. Here are some to consider.

1. He claimed to be the only way as in John's record 14:6 says but validation came through miracles that proved he was who he claimed to be.
2. Eyewitnesses saw Jesus' miracles and validated them as authentic. Over 500 followers saw Jesus, after his resurrection, and watched him ascend into heaven.
3. The prophets foretold of his coming, where he would be born, that he would be God in human flesh and lots more…all prophetic statements were realized in Jesus, even those like in Isaiah chapter 53 that were uttered hundreds of years before Jesus came.
4. God himself validated Jesus as his sole pathway to him. "While he was still speaking, behold, a bright cloud overshadowed them; and suddenly a voice came out of the cloud, saying, "This is My Beloved Son, in whom I am well pleased. Hear Ye Him!"(Mathew 17:5)
5. The apostles lost their homes, wealth, and even their lives preaching the gospel. Would they do that if it were a lie? I don't think so. They testified to the truth and were willing to die for it if necessary. (See Foxes Book of Martyrs)
6. Thousands of believers, over several centuries have testified of how Jesus helped them and blessed them.
7. I can personally testify that I have seen the hand of the Lord in my life and communicate with him daily. I know he is the Christ.

The provability that one man could fulfill all prophecies about a Messiah that God himself said would come, (Gen. 3:15), and perform fantastic miracles while here on earth, and be raised from the dead, and ascend into heaven while hundreds looked on is astronomical is astronomic. But Jesus did just that…fulfilled everything that was foretold about the coming Messiah. He had to be who he said he was and therefore is truly the only way to God.

Question: How does my salvation overcome the attacks of the devil? The answer is in the Bible. God is calling all of us to himself so we can be set free from sin, death and the wiles of the devil. If we do not rely on him, we are not blessed and protected.

Here's a scripture that explains it further. "The angel of the LORD encampeth round about them that fear him, and delivereth them." Psalm 34:7 The key to being protected is to fear (reverence) the Lord. When you do, his angel sets up his camp, that is filled with waring angels, all around you. Those that do not believe do not reverence and therefore do not qualify for The Angel of The Lord's Campfire.

You may be saying, "The Bible is just a book and not a final authority." Let's look at this more closely.

The Bible As The Final Authority

I use the Bible as my main source to validate all that I say. But most people, including Christians, do not read the Bible with any regularity and therefore do not know the God of the Bible. They know only what their pastor or others tell them. Here's a brief history lesson.

The history of the Bible starts with a phenomenal account, the creation of all things. It's not one book like many think -- It's an ancient collection of writings, comprised of 66 separate books, written over approximately 1,600 years, by at least 40 distinct authors. The Old Testament contains 39 books written from approximately 1500 BC to 400 BC, and the New Testament contains 27 books written from approximately 40 to 90 AD. The Jewish Bible (*Tanakh*) is the same as the Christian Old Testament, except for its book arrangement. The original Old Testament was written mainly in Hebrew, with some Aramaic, while the original New Testament was written in common Greek.

Starting in about 40 AD, and continuing to about 90 AD, the eyewitnesses to the life of Jesus, including Matthew, Mark, Luke, John, Paul, James, Peter and Jude, wrote the Gospels and letters that eventually became the Bible's New Testament. These authors quote from 31 books of the Old Testament. They widely circulated their material so that by about 150 AD, early Christians were referring to the entire set of writings as the "New Covenant." During the 200s AD, the original writings were translated from Greek into Latin, Coptic (Egypt) and Syriac (Syria), and widely disseminated as "Inspired Scripture" throughout the Roman Empire and beyond. In 397 AD, in an effort to protect the scriptures from various heresies and offshoot religious movements, the current 27 books of the New Testament were formally and finally confirmed and "canonized" in the Synod of Carthage.

What I hope you will see from this snapshot of the Bible in history is that God took great pains to validate his Word to man over many years, keeping it clear, and indisputable as the only true source of his revelation. These eyewitness accounts and prophetic revelations all connect to make a complete proof of God's existence, character, power, love, salvation, judgment, compassion, mercy and forgiveness. His entire plan of salvation and the ages to come is all written down so we could benefit from them.

Time and time again I have asked the Lord questions and found the answers in the Bible. I can remember one in particular. I was attending a small Christian fellowship that met in a barn. The leadership was teaching that God's judgment upon America was to come soon and that they could escape it by leaving the states and going to a remote desert-like place in another country. Several families had already moved to this undisclosed location. I was a very young believer and not as knowledgeable as I am now in the scriptures… so I turned to Jesus and asked him if these people were correct and if I should go with them. Here's what I read during my prayer and Bible reading.

Mathew 24:26 "Wherefore if they shall say unto you, Behold, he is in the desert; go not forth: behold, he is in the secret chambers; believe it not."

This is just one example of many that God has communicated to me through the Bible. Try it…when you are troubled, confused or worried about life or just need an answer to life's never ending questions, pray and ask Jesus to show you in his Word, the Bible.

The Bible was written under "Inspiration" from the Holy Spirit. The word, "inspire" means "To breathe upon or into something". God revealed himself through individuals who penned the written word.

As a young Christian, I often witnessed to non-believers, using the Bible as my source. Some of those I talked to told me that the Bible was not a source they would believe. I went to my pastor and asked him what I should do because folks were not open to hear what the Bible had to say. He led me to Hebrews 4:12 and said. "Use it anyway," for the reasons stated in chapter four. Listen to what it says. "For the word of God is quick, and powerful, and sharper than any two-edged sword, piercing even to the dividing asunder of soul and spirit, and of the joints and marrow, and is a discerner of the thoughts and intents of the heart." (Hebrews 4:12) I did just that and began to see the words of the Bible break down barriers and soften hearts.

I know that anyone who is really seeking God and wants to know about Jesus will find everything in the Bible. Words will leap off the page, bringing fresh revelation, historical facts, wisdom, divine counsel and victory over life's every trial. All you have to do is spend some time every day in prayer and Bible reading.

Tricks of The Devil

Satan has many tricks and plays them on humans all the time.

www.beliefnet.com Offers Six tricks or lies that are meant to capture your soul and leave you helplessly void of God's grace. I have chosen five to use in my book. Here they are:

1. **That Happiness Is Unattainable**

The devil wants you to stress about things outside of your control so that you don't rely on Christ, the One who strengthens, but that you will rely on the Enemy, the one who will do everything in his power to make you doubt all forms of joy and happiness. He wants you confused, anxious, and even angry about your life circumstances so that you will eventually become distant from God, and rely on your own understanding.

Read more at http://www.beliefnet.com/Faiths/Galleries/6-Things-the-Devil-Will-Trick-You-into-Believing.aspx?p=2#140xM9X7WlWr5FyS.99

2. **That God's Word Isn't Real**

The devil wants to trick you into believing the Bible is a collection of myths, in hopes that you will doubt God's Word and even His existence. He also wants you to believe that the Bible, written nearly 3500 years ago is no longer relevant in our modern world because it was written so long ago. But God's Word is real and has real significance. Not only was it written by more than 40 different writers over a 1600-year span with remarkable consistency, it explains life and the human experience in a way no other book has or ever will.

Read more at http://www.beliefnet.com/Faiths/Galleries/6-Things-the-Devil-Will-Trick-You-into-Believing.aspx?p=3#Ai6oWQMIeRswSOLI.99

3. **That You Aren't Significant**

While God wants you to live a life filled with purpose, the devil wants the opposite. He doesn't want you to think or care about your thoughts, attitude, words or actions and will trick you into believing you aren't significant. If he gets you to believe your life is without purpose, then you will live a life of sin, out of tune with God. But your life is significant. God knew you before you were even born. Remember, He knows the plans He has for you, plans to prosper you and not to harm you, plans to give you hope and a future (Jeremiah 29:11).

Read more at http://www.beliefnet.com/Faiths/Galleries/6-Things-the-Devil-Will-Trick-You-into-Believing.aspx?p=4#jdKQfLADEkhkJmQK.99

4. That Gossip Does No Harm, And Your Words Can't Hurt

The devil wants you to spread gossip and bad news so that you will focus on the negative and not believe in God's goodness or his blessings. If he tricks you into thinking gossip does no harm, you will then believe there's nothing wrong in spreading harmful or malicious words which can hurt the people you love, and allow you to develop a negative view of the world around you, which has an impact on all that you do.

Read more at http://www.beliefnet.com/Faiths/Galleries/6-Things-the-Devil-Will-Trick-You-into-Believing.aspx?p=6#O1jqXrjxaOeOZ7Bm.99

5. That The Physical World Outweighs the Spiritual World

If the devil can get you to believe the physical world is more real than the spiritual world, he can trick you into pursuing things like money, power and fame and have you believing that materialistic things are more important than being in a relationship with God. If you think this, then you won't seek first the kingdom of God. But there is far more greatness in God's Heavenly Kingdom than any material possession we acquire while in physical form on earth. Remember, earth is now. Heaven is forever.

Read more at http://www.beliefnet.com/Faiths/Galleries/6-Things-the-Devil-Will-Trick-You-into-Believing.aspx?p=7#jdpfcEDktTQbly7P.99

Weapons of Our Warfare

It's obvious that we need to know what our weapons are and how to use them…so lets look at some spiritual weapons. (For the weapons of our warfare *are* not carnal, but mighty through God to the pulling down of strong holds;) We will 1st look at the Armor Of God as presented in Ephesians 6:13-17.

"Therefore, take up the full armor of God, so that you will be able to resist in the evil day, and having done everything, to stand firm. Stand Firm therefore, Having Girded Your Loins With Truth, and Having Put on The Breastplate of Righteousness, and Having Shod Your Feet With The Preparation of the Gospel of Peace; in addition to all, taking up The Shield of Faith with which you will be able to extinguish all the flaming arrows of the *evil one*. And take the Helmet of Salvation, and the Sword of the Spirit, which is the Word of God."

So, we have Truth, Righteousness, Peace, Faith, Salvation and the Word of God or Bible…Six weapons, five defensive and one offensive. This represents the full armor of God to be worn and used so that we can resist in the evil day.

The evil day is the hour of temptation when Satan seeks to deceive us and draw us away from God. It is also when fiery darts are flung at us by demons. The deceptions are suggestive in nature that contradict God's will but seem logical such as, "everybody's doing it. It must be ok" or "drugs can't really hurt you." The fiery darts are insults like, "You're not good enough", "Not worth anything",

"Never amount to anything"…all are negative in nature that are meant to cause a low self-esteem, depression and even suicide.

The Sword of the Spirit is really cool because it's fashioned from over 3,000 promises of God…things like; "You are accepted in the beloved" Ephesians 1:6, "I am crucified with Christ: nevertheless I live; yet not I, but Christ lives in me: and the life which I now live in the flesh I live by the faith of the Son of God, who loved me, and gave himself for me." Galatians 2:20

"Nay, in all these things we are more than conquerors through him that loved us." Romans 8:37

All of Satan's efforts are designed to establish strongholds in our lives. How many has he established in you? What's a stronghold? Try these on for size: Over eating, drugs, smoking, anger, homosexuality, pornography, and all of the deeds of the flesh listed in Galatians chapter five. He'll try and try until he gets you hooked on some sort of vice. If you follow him, he takes you deeper and deeper into it until a stronghold is built which is really an outpost for demonic activity. Not to worry because the Sword of the Spirit can cut that evil stronghold into pieces and bring its efforts to naught.

K. N. O. B. S.

As a young Christian, I learned an acrostic that helped me to remember my primary weapons.

K = Knowledge Of God…" Casting down imaginations, and every high thing that exalteth itself against the knowledge of God, and bringing into captivity every thought to the obedience of Christ;" II Corinthians 10:5

Note: Anything that sets itself against what you know to be true, you cast it down and away from you.

N = Name Of Jesus… "That at the name of Jesus every knee should bow, of *things* in heaven, and *things* in earth, and *things* under the earth;" Philippians 2:10

Note: We can use our lord's name to stop the evil attack. Say it out loud if need be…"I cast you out and bind your influence from me, In The Name of Jesus, be gone.

O = Obedience… "And bringing into captivity every thought to the obedience of Christ;" II Corinthians 10:5

Note: we are to bring every thought into captivity. In other words… hold every thought against the truth of the Word of God to be sure it is not a deception or trap.

B = Blood Of Christ …" If we confess our sins, he is faithful and just to forgive us *our* sins, and to cleanse us from all unrighteousness."

Note: through confession, His blood can cleanse us from our sin. That means when Satan accuses us, we can put it under the blood in confession before the throne of God and know it will fade away. Satan will try to use it anyway but we can stand against it, saying we've been forgiven.

S = Sword Of The Spirit… "For the word of God *is* quick, and powerful, and sharper than any two-edged sword, piercing even to the dividing asunder of soul and spirit, and of the joints and marrow, and *is* a discerner of the thoughts and intents of the heart." **Hebrews 4:12 Note:** We can use the Word of God to fight back. It will always win.

Other "Word" Weapons

Consider these:
- **Give No Place To The Devil**…"Neither give place to the devil." Ephesians 4:27

Note: The best thing you can do is do not argue, negotiate, compromise or allow any negative or suggestive thoughts into your mind.

- **Prayer & Praise….** "Let God arise, let his enemies be scattered: let them also that hate him flee before him. As smoke is driven away, so drive them away: as wax melts before the fire, so let the wicked perish at the presence of God." Psalm 68:1 & 2

Note: Prayer always works as a weapon and when you add praise, you have a powerful combination that Satan cannot overcome.

- **Trust In The Lord At All Times**…"Trust in the LORD with all your heart and lean not on your own understanding; in all your ways submit to him, and he will make your paths straight." Proverbs 3:5-6

Note: Too many folks worry, cry and cuss over their circumstances. Learning to trust requires an absolute allegiance to Jesus, knowing he will direct you in and through every situation.

- **All Things Work Together For Good…**" And we know that all things work together for good to them that love God, to them who are the called according to his purpose." Romans 8:28

Note: Here's a great weapon because its foundation is the knowledge that God has a master plan and he is always working everything together for good in the lives of those who are called to salvation, all those, "Whosoevers" of **John 3:16** who love the Lord. If that is you, you can know that God is ever in your background, making thing right.

- **Let The Peace of God Be The Referee**…"And let the peace of God rule in your hearts, to **the** which also ye are called in one body; and be ye thankful." Colossians 3:16

Note: If we can allow the peace of God to rule in our hearts, it will keep out all the clutter that Satan tries to fill our minds with. It's another great weapon in defensive warfare.

- **Stand Fast...**"Stand fast therefore in the liberty wherewith Christ hath made us free, and be not entangled again with the yoke of bondage" Galatians 5:1

Note: With all of the above weapons available to us, we should not fear Satan. He is a defeated foe. He has to steal your power to have any of his own. If we treat him accordingly, as a defeated foe, by standing fast to our confession of faith in Jesus and applying the scriptures against his attacks, we will no doubt remain peaceful, happy and free to serve our Lord.

I am sure that you'll find more weapons. Our salvation set us free from the bondage of sin. Going back into that lifestyle is just not an option. We need to recognize the battle, learn about our enemy and use the weapon of choice to fit the attack. Failing to fight is to lose before you start and settle for a life in captivity.

Fighting Demonic Spirits

When we discuss fighting demonic spirits, it is easy to fall into error. One error is that we begin to believe that there's a demon behind every situation. That is just not so. It is easy to say, *"The devil Made Me Do It"* instead of owning up to our own lust, anger or other failures.

People have a "Free Will" to make decisions and they often times use poor judgment and make wrong decisions that can affect others. Blaming demons is popular because it hides the evil in our own hearts. "The heart is deceitful above all things, and desperately wicked: who can know it" Jeremiah 17:9

Jesus said, "Not that which goes into the mouth defiles a man, but that which cometh out of the mouth, this defiles a man." Mathew 15:11 So blaming evil forces for what we do is not religiously correct.

The other error in fighting demonic influences is...not believing that demonic activity is real and that it never affects you. Jesus cast out demons. His disciples did also and for centuries the church has faced demonic activity.

Here's a partial list of situations that might indicate that you are under demonic control or attack.

- Thinking thoughts "that are not you."
- Having sudden depression.
- Having suicidal thoughts.
- Having fits of anger or rage that are unusual for you.
- Feeling hopeless.
- Your pets start acting differently around you.
- Your close friends start questioning your thinking or behavior.
- Excessive fatigue.
- Not being able to do what you know is good or right.
- Feeling like you are being pulled to do the wrong thing.
- Feeling like you are being pressured to do something you don't want to do.
- Hearing voices or thoughts in your head that are negative, persuasive, or commanding you to do something.
- Deep or severe personality changes like fear or wanting to be isolated all the time.
- Suddenly having creepy or scary feelings.
- Recent feelings that an area, like in your house, there is something heavy, depressive or oppressive.

- Feelings of being under attack or threatened when others don't.
- Finding it hard or impossible to pray.
- Finding it harder or impossible to spend time with Christian brothers or sisters.
- Sudden and unexplainable anxiety.
- Sudden development of Lupus or other auto immune system disease.

Some medical problems can cause similar conditions. It could be from a new bad habit or an encounter with a sinful situation or circumstance. If this is true, you know what to do. Repent and move on with your life. Trust Jesus. (The above list is an excerpt from Pastor Thomas of The Joseph Plan World Wide Ministry) ministry@thejosephplan.org

The best way to dispel demonic activity in your life is to call upon the name of the Lord and command that demon to leave you, *in the name of Jesus*. Then draw close to God, through prayer and seek his divine revelation as to what to do next.

He will most likely send you to the Bible to read and listen as he speaks to you from the pages of the Bible. You will get all the direction you need to overcome a demonic influence.

Remember, resist the devil and he will flee from you. To resist is to quote scripture, as Jesus did in the wilderness.

Why Me Lord?

If you are like me, you probably said, *"Why Me Lord"* There was a time when I thought I could be neutral, just doing my own thing but still believing in God. The problem with that sort of thinking is that can not be.

We were created to be the image and likemess of God here on this earth. God went to a lot of trouble to create and enact a plan that would accomplish this. With the fall of Adam and the entire human race, we were left with being the image of Satan. Now our "Free Will" choice is to stay with the deeds of the flesh, which is the nature of evil or to be, "Born Again" and receive the Spirit of God. There is no neutral ground.

There are some believers that feel that if they have a lot of faith they will not undergo any suffering, severe tests or satanic attacks. Nothing could be further from the truth! Actually, the opposite is true.

I Peter 5:8-9 teaches that Satan roams the earth seeking someone to devour. When we read the context, we can come to the conclusion that the devil's main focus is to thwart, divert, distract and disarm the servants of God who are promoting the rule of God on the earth as it is in heaven. Heaven is the only realm in the universe where everything is perfectly aligned under King Jesus, since the devil was displaced from there (Rev. 12:7-12).

Consequently, when someone on earth wants to bring the influence of the kingdom of God on earth as it is in heaven, Satan erupts with fear and anger against them since he doesn't want to be thrown out of another place!

This is why it seems as though a person following the will of God will sometimes have the most difficult tests, trials and resistance, as opposed to some saints who are casual seekers. The casual seeker is already being controlled through the deeds of the flesh.

Satan is no dummy. Why should he attack a Christian who is a bad example to others and who is already deceived and in his grip? He will focus the most on those who are the biggest threats to his desire, to do a power grab from God over the earthly realm!

Remember: God gave Adam a commission to rule over the whole

earth (Gen. 1:28), and immediately after that the devil came and convinced both Adam and Eve to disobey God and abandon their posts as God's vice regents over the earth (Gen. 3:1-8).

Since that time Satan has been jealously attempting to protect his control over the earthly realm that he stole through subverting Adam, including its systems of government, commerce, media, the arts, science and education.

So, if you are sold out for God, don't be discouraged when you are attacked or allow yourself to be deceived into thinking that the only reason you are in intense spiritual warfare or tribulation is because you may have missed God. It may be the opposite. You are being targeted because you are hitting the divine bull's eye! This is why Paul admonished believers to stand strong in the Lord:

"Our struggle is not against flesh and blood but against principalities, powers and the rulers of darkness in high places" (Ephesians 6:10-13). Notice: Paul said "our struggle" meaning he was including himself in this struggle. Every time there was an open door for ministry he had many adversaries. This is a biblical principle. (read 1 Corinthians 16:9)

Do not ever think that just because God is calling you to do something that it will be easy. Jesus did the will of God and he was crucified, and church history tells us Paul was beheaded! It's not how many years we live, but what we do with the years we live that matters!

So, what do we do when we are in a time of spiritual warfare that Paul calls "the day of evil" in Ephesians 6:13? Paul tells us in this passage to be strong in the Lord and to stand firm; in other words, do not quit (Eph. 6:10-13).

The apostle Peter also tells us to resist the devil, standing firm in the faith (1 Pet. 5:9). Peter knows firsthand that faith in God is the key to standing firm in the midst of the day of evil because, when he denied Christ three times, Jesus prayed for him that his "faith" would not fail (Luke 22:31-32).

So, do not be afraid when you are in tribulation, because Jesus has already overcome the world (John 16:33)!

What To Do Next?

The Bible gives us clear instruction on how to keep ourselves free, healthy and happy in a world that is a battleground where Satan seeks to kill, steal and destroy. (John 10:10) Here's a recap of what we can do next to keep our hearts:

Be transformed-…Romans 12:2; *Cast down imaginations-*…2 Corinthians 10:5; *Bring into captivity every thought to the obedience of Christ;* 2 Corinthians 10:5; *Be spiritually minded-*Romans 8:6; *Put off the old man-*Ephesians 4:22; *Be renewed in your mind-*Ephesians 4:23; *Put on the new man-*Ephesians 4:24; *Let the mind of Christ be in you-* Philippians 5; *Let no man beguile you-*Colossians 2:18; *Let no man spoil you-*Colossians 2:8; *Be fully persuaded in your mind-*Romans 14:5; *Do not have a doubtful mind-*Luke 12:29; *Do not be soon shaken in mind-*2 Thessalonians 2:2; *Do not Be troubled-*2 Thessalonians 2:2; *Gird up the loins of your mind-*1 Peter 1:13; *Be sober-*1 Peter 1:13 and *Hope to the end for the grace of God-*1 Peter.

I am sure you will find more things as you read the scripture but these will make a great starting place. Just remember, God is always with you. He is not mad at you, nor does he expect you to win every time. Your salvation does not hang in the balance. If you fail, He will just pick you up and help you along the way until you can sit, walk and run.

Signs of The End of The Age
And The Rise of Satanic Influences

We have all been told that the end of the world is at hand. Hollywood has even made movies on how it might happen. I want to show some of the rise of satanic influences and how it will affect us. Let's first look at what Jesus said about the end times as recorded in Matthew 24.

"See that no one leads you astray. *For many will come in my name, saying, 'I am ͨthe Christ,' and they will lead many astray.* And you will hear of wars and rumors of wars. See that you are not alarmed, for this must take place, but the end is not yet. For nation will rise against nation, and kingdom against kingdom, and there will be famines and earthquakes in various places. All these are but the beginning of the birth pains." Matthew 24:4-8

"And many false prophets will arise ᵖand lead many astray. And because lawlessness will be increased, the love of many will grow cold: Matthew 24: 11-12. "For false Christs and false prophets will arise and perform great signs and wonders, so as to lead astray, if possible, even the elect." Matthew 24:24

"Let no man deceive you by any means: for that day shall not come, *except there come a falling away first*, and that man of sin be revealed, the son of perdition: II Thessalonians 2:3

Here's what I see in these scriptures

1. Many will come in his name saying that they are Christ. This, in my opinion, refers to false Christians as well as false teachers. They say they are of the Christian Faith but do not follow the doctrine that the apostles taught. The Mormons call themselves Latter Day Saints and have changed the gospel to fit their own perspectives. They are deceiving many and taking them away from the true Gospel.
2. Other groups, known as the Occults do the same thing.
3. Modern day churches, both Protestant and Catholic are full of folks that example doctrine of devils, yet they claim to be Christians.

It is obvious that false prophets have come onto the world stage, as though they were a "Pied Piper", and they have led many astray. It is also obvious that there has been, over the last 50 years, a great falling away from the faith and doctrines taught by Jesus and his disciples.

I said all of that to say this. The same demons that led many to follow false prophets to believe in doctrines of devils are still here, hard at work, to take you down. We need to recognize what is happening around us. We need to discern the times we live in and we need to discover and apply the weapons of our warfare so we do not get lost in the crowd that is being led astray.

The battle of the ages is for the souls of mankind. It all takes place in the minds of every human being. Before wars break out between countries, battles are fought and lost in the minds of the leaders of those nations. To survive in a life and death struggle for our soul, we will absolutely need to be able to recognize our enemy, know his dirty tricks and schemes, and what weapons God has provided for us to defend ourselves and even win the battle.

We will need to realize that Jesus has defeated every evil force and given us power over them. We need to know that this battle of the ages is the Lords. He knows exactly what to do, when to do it and who to send into the battle to take back what the devil has stolen.

In other words, He has a master plan that is being worked out in the earth. All we need to do is trust Him, believe his Word, apply His counsel and rest in his finished work of Grace.

I hope this chapter has helped you to understand and to motivate you to become a partner with Christ in the Battle of The Ages.

CHAPTER EIGHT

LIFE AT THE END OF THE AGE

So far, I have discussed the times leading up to the end. We had to start at the beginning so we could understand why there is an end.

This chapter will be a study of end times. If we do not consider this topic, we do ourselves a grave injustice because the time will come and it could be in our lifetime. It is better to examine the scriptural references and draw our conclusions now rather than think it will not happen, be unprepared and fall into despair.

How do you prepare for total destruction? As I talk with others about the end of times, all I get is Fear, Skepticism and Confusion. No one has a clear-cut answer and everyone seems to have his or her own opinion.

Our study will examine the Skeptic's view, the Theologian's view and the person on the street. We'll discover facts, theories and Biblical views of what may very well be our own end of days.

The Big Event

There can be no bigger event in the history of this world than its total destruction. It may even be bigger than its creation. God created it and plans to destroy it. The question is, when? Other questions also exist like: Will I be living when it happens? Can I know before time approximately when it will occur? Is there anything I can do to delay it or stop it from happening? What will life be like in the years just before and as that final moment comes?

Important Terms

Presented by: B.A. Robinson

Eschatology is a Christian term that means the study of the end of history from a religious perspective. Probably more obscure theological text has been written on this topic than on any other belief in Christendom.

The Bible contains many prophecies about the future. The Christian Scriptures (New Testament) in particular, talks extensively about the return of Jesus Christ to this earth. This is usually called his "second coming," or "parousia." The Gospel of Matthew, Chapter 24, is devoted to this topic, as is much of the book of Revelation, and 1 Thessalonians 4:16-18. A *literal* interpretation of the Bible shows that four important events are predicted:

The Millennium: Revelation describes an important interval lasting for 1000 years when Christ rules on earth free of sin and Satan. We will rule with him. This is a golden era; a time of universal peace.

The Tribulation: This is a 7-year interval when a world religious-political leader called the Anti-Christ takes power.

Armageddon: This is a terrible war provoked by the Anti-Christ. Most people on earth will die. God's wrath will be poured out over evil people who are on the earth at this time. A series of violent events are predicted in Daniel 9, Matthew 24, and Revelation 4-19.

The Rapture: 1 Thessalonians 4:16-18 describes an event when Christ will descend from the heavens towards the earth. Many conservative protestants believe that faithful *"born again"* Christians who have previously died will be resurrected, (rise from their graves), and ascend to meet Jesus in the sky. Immediately afterwards, *"born again"* Christians who had not died will also ascend into the air to be with the Lord.

Teaching on the End Times (Eschatology) is important:

- It makes up some 9% of the New Testament, which is a very significant proportion.
- The New Testament teaches that we should be living in the light of the End Times.
- It is important that the Christian community has an informed hope, instead of the current ignorance or fear.
- It is important that the Christian community has a proper sense of accountability to God including an awareness of the last judgment.

Discerning The Signs of The Times "Life Before The End"

So, according to Matthew 24, here's what will happen as we draw closer and closer to the "Big Event" which is the end of all things. These are the signs of the times that tell us if we are really in the last days before Jesus comes back and whether or not we are fast approaching the end of days.

1. Many shall come on the scene saying, I am Christ;(or I am a Christian) and shall deceive many.
2. We will hear of wars and rumors of wars.
3. Nation will rise against nation, and kingdom against kingdom.
4. There will be famines, and pestilences, and earthquakes, in divers places.
5. Many will be offended, and shall betray one another, and shall hate one another.

6. Many false prophets will rise, and shall deceive many.
7. The love of many shall wax cold.
8. And this gospel of the kingdom shall be preached in the entire world for a witness unto all nations.
9. As the days of Noah were, so will be the days before Jesus returns.

Life After The Tribulation

These are prophetic revelations of what is about to happen but are scheduled on God's timeline for after the great tribulation.

1. The powers of the heavens shall be shaken.
2. The sun be darkened, and the moon shall not give her light.
3. The stars shall fall from heaven.
4. The sign of the Son of man in heaven.
5. The heavens being on fire shall be dissolved.
6. The elements shall melt with fervent heat.

Does your future look bright? It should because God's purpose in revealing his plans through the prophets and Jesus and his apostles is to increase our hope and strengthen our faith.

Peter said, *"Seeing then that all these things shall be dissolved, what manner of persons ought ye to be in all holy conversation and godliness, Looking for and hasting unto the coming of the day of God, wherein the heavens being on fire shall be dissolved, and the elements shall melt with fervent heat?"*

Because we know that the end of the world is at hand, we are sure to live in the light of that knowledge. That would be using holy conversation and seeking to walk in a godly lifestyle. This is why we are pre-warned. God does not want us to be caught unaware.

Suddenly And Without Warning

Jesus said about his return to earth that life would be like it was in the days of Noah before the flood. "And as it was in the days of Noah, so shall it be also in the days of the Son of man. They did eat, they drank, they married wives, they were given in marriage, until the day that Noah entered into the ark, and the flood came, and destroyed them all." Luke 17:26-27 (without warning was because they did not want to listen or obey. Thus, they were taken by total surprise.)

The Cause And Effect Scenario

One powerful example of cause and effect occurred in the time of Noah. The book of Genesis makes clear that "the wickedness of man was great in the earth, and that every intent of the thoughts of man's heart was only evil continually" (Genesis 6:5). The world then was "filled with violence," as humans corrupted themselves and God's creation (Genesis 6:11).

This disobedience to God's beneficial laws caused automatic pain and suffering to the point that God was "grieved in his heart" and decided to start all over again through Noah and his family (verses 6, 18).

Even though, from God's perspective, the storm clouds of the impending flood were obvious, the people of Noah's day ignored Noah's warnings and lived as if nothing were wrong. Jesus Christ made this point in his warning to people about the signs of the end time. He said…

"For as in the days before the flood, they were eating and drinking, marrying and giving in marriage, until the day that Noah entered the ark, and did not know until the flood came and took them all away, so also will the coming of the Son of Man be" (Matthew 24:38-39).

Year after year, human opinions about sin have changed. Actions recognized as wrong in the past are increasingly accepted, whether premarital sex, cheating, lying, swearing, lusting or homosexuality. Jesus warned that we must not fall prey to the apathy of Noah's day.

The Day of The Lord

What's being said? Only This …life was as normal as ever. There were no real signs that warned the people. It just happened and when it did, it was too late. "But the day of the Lord will come as a thief in the night; in which the heavens shall pass away with a great noise, and the elements shall melt with fervent heat, the earth also and the works that are therein shall be burned up." II Peter 3:10

I know, Jesus was asked about what was the sign of his coming. Then shall appear the sign of the Son of Man. What is that sign?

The Unveiling of Shekinah Glory

Revelation 6 says people scream for the rocks and the mountains to cover them up and hide them from the face of the One who sits on the throne, the One who comes in blazing glory. And I believe it's none other than the Lord himself. That's the sign. It is the revelation of the Son of Man in heaven. In the midst of this blackness will appear in blazing, infinite, unveiled glory, the Son of Man. In fact, at the end of verse 30, it says He will come not just with glory but with great glory. Glory like the world has never seen.

Some of the disciples received a glimpse of this glory. Matthew 17 describes the transfiguration of Jesus. Jesus took James, Peter and John up to the mountain, pulled aside the veil of his flesh, and they beheld his glory, and they got a taste of what second coming Shekinah was like. And it was only a small one and Peter never forgot it, and remember when he penned II Peter, he said we have not come unto you with cunningly devised fables, we don't tell you lies invented by men, we were eyewitnesses of his majesty when we were with him in the holy mount. We got a glimpse of second coming glory. (Excerpts from John Mc Arthur of Grace To You)

The word, **"Shekinah"** is a Hebrew word that means the presence of God on earth or a symbol or manifestation of his presence.

Remember the unveiled glory of Jesus, as it is in heaven will not appear until the great tribulation is over with all its destruction, the sun and moon shines no more, the heavens shaken, and the stars falling. Then, in the midst of all this chaos, Jesus opens the heavens so those who are left see him seated in the heavens.

Two Key Signs
One For You & One For Them

It's important to see that life is as usual before and up to the great tribulation. There are no signs it see. Hear what the apostle John says, "even now are there many antichrists; whereby we know that it is the last time." I John 2:18 This is how we know that we are living in the last days…because of the many "Anti-Christs" that are in the world.

The other sign is the revelation of the Son of Man in heaven. The unveiling of his Shekinah Glory to this world. After the tribulation came the sign of his coming, being the glory he exhibits in heaven and will here on the earth.

There are signs everywhere but the two mentioned above are the most important because of what they tell us.

Sign #1…**Multiple Anti-Christ**s…The earth is full of antichrists that are hard at work trying to mislead the human race and Christians in particular. Have you noticed any Anti-Christs lately? The one thing they do that gives them away as being an, "Anti-Christ" is…well I'll let John tell you, "1 John 4:2 Hereby know ye the Spirit of God: Every spirit that confesses that Jesus Christ is come in the flesh is of God: 1 John 4:3 And every spirit that confesses not that Jesus Christ is come in the flesh is not of God: and this is that spirit of Anti-Christ, whereof ye have heard that it should come; and even now already is it in the world. II John 1:7 For many deceivers are entered into the world, who confess not that Jesus Christ is come in the flesh. This is a deceiver and an Anti-Christ.

Sign #2… Shekinah Glory…, which we have already discussed. However, note that sign #1 is for us along with all the other signs. Sign #2 is a warning to those who are alive after the tribulation. This is pictured in Revelation 6:16, "And said to the mountains and rocks, Fall on us, and hide us from the face of him that sitteth on the throne, and from the wrath of the Lamb:"

God's Exit Strategy
For Those Living At The End of Days

Considering that all these things happen during and after the great tribulation of those days, where are the saints? As we have already discussed, they were caught up together in the clouds to join the Lord in the air and so they shall be with him forever.

"For God hath not appointed us to wrath, but to obtain salvation by our Lord Jesus Christ, who died for us, that, whether we wake or sleep, we should live together with him. Wherefore comfort yourselves together, and edify one another, even as also ye do." I Thessalonians 5:9-11

The 1st century saints were admonished to take comfort in the fact that God had not appointed them to wrath. The great tribulation is when God pours out his wrath upon the earth.

Here is another few passages to look at from II Thessalonians, chapter two.

"That ye be not soon shaken in mind, or be troubled, neither by spirit, nor by word, nor by letter as from us, as that the day of Christ is at hand. Let no man deceive you by any means: for that day shall not come, except there come a falling away first, and that man of sin be revealed, the son of perdition; Who opposeth and exalteth himself above all that is called God, or that is worshipped; so that he as God sitteth in the temple of God, shewing himself that he is God. Remember ye not, that, when I was yet with you, I told you these things? And now ye know what withholdeth that he might be revealed in his time. For the mystery of iniquity doth already work: only he who now letteth will let, until he be taken out of the way.

And then shall that "Wicked One" be revealed, whom the Lord shall consume with the spirit of his mouth, and shall destroy with the brightness of his coming: Even him, whose coming is after the working of Satan with all power and signs and lying wonders, And with all deceivableness of unrighteousness in them that perish; because they received not the love of the truth, that they might be saved.

And for this cause God shall send them strong delusion, that they should believe a lie: that they all might be damned who believed not the truth, but had pleasure in unrighteousness."

Note: God's wrath is to be poured upon those who take pleasure in unrighteousness, not those that love and serve the Lord. God will even send them a strong delusion to be sure they will not repent.

One More Thought... This is worth saying again..."For the mystery of iniquity doth already work: only he who now letteth will let, until he be taken out of the way." II Thessalonians 2:7

He that letteth (or Restrains) is the Holy Spirit of God. Until he is taken out of the way, he will continue to restrain the full expression of evil in human flesh from appearing. Because Jesus said he would never leave us comfortless but would be with us even to the end of the age, it only makes sense that when he, the Holy Spirit, is taken, we will be taken with him. To leave us and take him would be abandonment and contrary to what Jesus said.

So, we will go with the Spirit when he goes and that will be before the Anti-Christ is revealed. This qualifies us to receive a Pre-Tribulation Exit. The wrath of God falls only after the Man of Sin is revealed.

Now Hear This! "For the Lord himself shall descend from heaven with a shout, with the voice of the archangel, and with the trump of God: and the dead in Christ shall rise first: Then we which are alive and remain shall be caught up together with them in the clouds, to meet the Lord in the air: and so shall we ever be with the Lord. Wherefore comfort one another with these words." This is the reason we are not to be so soon shaken, fearful, full of doubt and anxious. Because God has made provisions for us so we won't suffer the wrath of God. Philippians 4:13

The End of The World Is At Hand

Most folks believe that the end of days is not far off. How far? Well that's another whole story. To say that it is "At Hand" is to say that it is imminent, about to happen or here now. Here are some weird predictions of the return of Jesus Christ which is synnonomus with end of days thinking.

1. Kenton Beshore Kyle, pastor of Mariners church in California, said Jesus Christ would come in the Rapture around 2021. There will then be seven years of tribulation – a period of intense suffering, which will end with Christ establishing a new kingdom.

2. The Messiah Foundation International says an asteroid will collide with the earth in this year, destroying it. Riaz Ahmed Gohar Shahi, founder of the organization, says the "mam-

moth comet" is already "hurtling" towards us. Also: followers believe Shahi's image is present on the moon.

3. The world will end for the fifth time in 2060, according to Sir Isaac Newton. The English physicist and mathematician used the Book of Daniel to come up with the date, according to a 1704 letter, which went on show in Jerusalem's Hebrew University in 2007.

The Anti-Christ

"For all that is in the world, the lust of the flesh, and the lust of the eyes, and the pride of life, is not of the Father, but is of the world. And the world passes away, and the lust thereof: but he that doeth the will of God abides forever.

Little children, *it is the last time*: and as ye have heard that Anti-Christ shall come, even now are there many Anti-Christs; whereby we know that it is the last time. They went out from us, but they were not of us; for if they had been of us, they would no doubt have continued with us: but they went out, that they might be made manifest that they were not all of us. But ye have an unction from the Holy One, and ye know all things.

I have not written unto you because ye know not the truth, but because ye know it, and that no lie is of the truth. Who is a liar but he that denies that Jesus is the Christ? He is Anti-Christ that denies the Father and the Son.

Whosoever denies the Son, the same hath not the Father: he that acknowledges the Son hath the Father also. Let that therefore abide in you, which ye have heard from the beginning. If that which ye have heard from the beginning shall remain in you, ye also shall continue in the Son, and in the Father. And this is the promise that he hath promised us, even eternal life. These things have I written unto you concerning them that seduce you.

But the anointing which ye have received of him abides in you, and ye need not that any man teach you: but as the same anointing teaches you of all things, and is truth, and is no lie, and even as it hath taught you, ye shall abide in him. And now, little children, abide in him; that, when he shall appear, we may have confidence, and not be ashamed before him at his coming." I John 2:16-28

We began our study seeking to discover life at the end of the age. There is that nagging question in everybody's mind that says," Will I be here on earth." If so, what can I expect?

By now it should be obvious that the answer lies in where you are spiritually.

Group #1...If you are being led by the Holy Spirit, he will walk with you through this life and when he departs, he will take you with him. You will experience the Pre-Tribulation exit. That experience is reserved for only those who have been, "Born Again"

Group #2...If you are not, "Born Again" you will be left behind when the Holy Spirit is taken out of the way. You will have to face the anger of the "Anti-Christ" as he takes over the world and dominates the human race. It will be a full manifestation of evil that the world has ever seen. You will be left to go through the 7-year tribulation and be forced to receive the mark of the beast or suffer dearly at the hands of evil spirits. Your only escape will be to reject the mark of the beast and seek salvation in Jesus. You will also have to overcome every thing the devil throws at you. You must endure until the every end. Good luck with that. It is possible for the scriptures tell us that a great multitude came out of the tribulation into the kingdom of God. They were converts of the 144,000 Jews that evangelized the world during that time.

Group #3...those left behind that follow after wickedness...those that rejected God to follow false gods, and those that would not submit to the will of God. The scripture says God will send them a great delusion so that they might be damned.

Group # 2 & 3 will not be invited to the Pre-Trib Exit but Group #2 will have a chance to be saved if they can endure until the end.

Group #3 has no hope after the exit of the Saints. However, simply confessing their sin to God, repenting and receiving Jesus into their hearts as Lord can save them all. It's not too late.

Which group are you in? When it's all over, Jesus will say these words. "Then shall the king say unto them (The Sheep) on his right hand, come, ye blessed of my Father, inherit the kingdom prepared for you from the foundation of the world:" Those on His left, (The Goats) well, they didn't make it. "Then shall he say also unto them on the left hand, depart from me, ye cursed, into everlasting fire, prepared for the devil and his angels:" (Matthew 25:34 & 41)

If you are Born Again, we will see you in the clouds as we rise up to meet the Lord in the air. If you are in one of the other groups, we, "Born Again" believers" will be watching to see if you are a sheep or a goat.

CHAPTER NINE

OVERCOMING THE ENEMY OF YOUR SOUL

THE RACE IS ON AND we are running out of time. The end of the world is almost here. Our goal is to arrive safely at the point of departure and observe God's wrath from a higher perspective, heaven. However, we are still in a battle of our own with the forces of evil as we walk towards the end of time.

Jesus said, as recorded in John 10:10, "The thief does not come except to steal, and to kill, and to destroy. I have come that they may have life, and that they may have *it* more abundantly. Peter said, "Be sober, be vigilant; because your adversary the devil walks about like a roaring lion, seeking whom he may devour." I Peter 5:8 Sadly enough, 40% of professing Christians do not believe in Satan as a real being, only a symbol of evil.

A 2009 nationwide survey of adults' spiritual beliefs, conducted by The Barna Group, suggests that Americans who consider themselves to be Christian have a diverse set of beliefs. Four out of ten Christians (40%) strongly agreed that Satan "is not a living being but is a symbol of evil."

I am here to tell you that Satan is a real being and he is after you, to steal, kill and destroy your soul. The soul is your mind, will and emotions. If he can influence you there, he can capture you and use you as his tool to hurt others. It all happens in the soul before it plays out in reality. A good example is how he can spin a lie and kill more than 60 million unborn babies. He just said that abortion is a women's health choice. It is not sin that murders innocent babies in the womb. That's the biggest lie I ever heard.

Did you know that there is a heartbeat within 13-19-day of conception? Yet in many states legal abortions can take place even in the last trimester, at full term.

How to Overcome Satan

The Enemy of Your Soul

Satan has many names but that is no matter. He is a defeated foe but yet very powerful. The sure way to win over such an evil force is to resist him steadfastly in the faith as I Peter 5:9 says. "Whom resist stedfast in the faith, knowing that the same afflictions are accomplished in your brethren that are in the world."

Your adversary, the devil, wants to establish strongholds in your life, through which he can control your emotions and manipulate your actions towards doing evil. These strongholds are in your mind. It is how you think about things, you perspective in life.

Before demonic strongholds can be overcome, we should understand exactly what demonic strongholds are. I said this before in a previous chapter but it is worth stating again so you get it. The word *stronghold* appears only once in the New Testament (2 Corinthians 10:4), and the Greek word translated "stronghold" means "a fortification such as a castle."

In this passage, the apostle Paul is instructing the church at Corinth on how to fight against and "destroy arguments and every lofty opinion raised against the knowledge of God" (2 Corinthians 10:5). They do this, not by using the weapons of the world, but by "divine power." Lofty arguments and opinions are the result of pride and evil and vain imaginations, the very strongholds in which demons reside. This, then, is the essence of demonic warfare—the power of God to overcome the strongholds of demons.

Practical Application of II Corinthians 10:5

We can use this scripture as a pathway to victory over evil no matter where it comes from. The key is to bring every thought into the light of the Word of God. Then cast down or reject everyone that sets itself above the Knowledge of God. You hold the thought captive and judge it by what you know is true from the scripture. This keeps you from acting upon thoughts that do not agree with God's will.

We can put our thoughts and what others tell us on trial. The key is… knowing what the Bible says. If you are not a student of the Bible, you'll never amass enough truth to be able to judge. This is a problem in the church today.

The Armor of God

In Ephesians 6:10-18, Paul describes the resources that God makes available to his followers—the armor of God. Here we are told how, in an attitude of humility and dependence, we are to avail ourselves of God's resources. Note that we are to be strong "in the Lord" and "in the power of his might."

We do not take on demonic strongholds in our own strength. We protect ourselves with the first five pieces of defensive armor and wield the one offensive weapon—the sword of the Spirit, which is the Word of God. We do all of this "with all kinds of prayers and requests . . . praying for all the Lord's people" (verse 18). In verses 12 and 13 of Ephesians 6, Paul writes, "For we do not wrestle against flesh and blood, but against principalities, against powers, against the rulers of the darkness of this age, against spiritual hosts of wickedness in the heavenly places. Therefore take up the whole armor of God, that you may be able to withstand in the evil day, and having done all, to stand."

One habit that every believer needs to develop is focusing on Ephesians 6:10–18 and "getting dressed" spiritually every day. It would go a long way to gaining victory over the devil and his schemes. Here Paul states that, while we walk in the flesh (we are living and breathing in this human body), we do not war according to the flesh (we can't fight spiritual battles with fleshly weapons). Instead, as we focus on the resources and weapons of spiritual strength, we can see God giving us victory. No demonic stronghold can withstand praying Christians wearing the full armor of God. We battle with the Word of God and are empowered by his Spirit.

CHAPTER TEN

DIVINE APPOINTMENTS

THE END OF DAYS IS at hand but life still goes on for us. We still follow Jesus along the way. Part of that following involves "Divine Appointments."

Have you ever experienced the blessings of God? Many of us have. In most cases, the blessing of God came as a result of some sort of divine appointment. God has a way of causing our path to cross the paths of others, some of which are used by God to bless us. If you've been walking with the Lord for a while, you will know that what I am saying is true.

I have had divine appointments with angels, with Godly men, with unsaved folks and even with evil forces. However, not everything that comes into our day is by divine direction. Much is due to the planting and harvesting effect of our own actions. Then there are the attacks of the devil and his fiery darts. Finally, there is the voice of the Holy Spirit and the ministry of the angels to the Saints.

Here are a few scriptures and\or thoughts to validate what I am saying.

Divine Appointments With Angels

- *"The angel of the LORD encamps round about them that fear him, and delivers them." Psalm 34:7*

I know that the angel of the lord comes with an entire camp of warring angels. They set up their perimeters all around us and are prepared at a moment's notice to deliver us. That is…if we fear (reverence) God. This is a divine appointment each time it happens.

- There are other occurrences that were recorded in the Bible. How about the time Gabriel, the angel, visited Mary… where the angel told her she would give birth to Jesus, even though she had never been with a man? (Story-Luke 1:26-35)

- How about when Peter was visited by an angel when he was in prison and the angel led him out of the prison with the doors still locks. (Story-Acts 12:1-25)

Divine Appointments With The Devil &/or Evil Spirits

- *"Then was Jesus led up of the Spirit into the wilderness to be tempted of the devil." Matthew 4:1*

Jesus had a divine appointment with the devil. His faith and loyalty to God had to be tested or purified. He faced the challenge and overcame the enemy using; "It Is Written," as a weapon.

The Spirit does not lead us into temptation. In fact, the Bible says God does not tempt man with evil. James 12:13, however, it is open season on Christians by evil forces and we encounter them everyday. Our weapon is the same as what Jesus used, "It Is Written"

- *"Be sober, be vigilant; because your adversary the devil, as a roaring lion, walks about, seeking whom he may devour: Whom resist stedfast in the faith, knowing that the same afflictions are accomplished in your brethren that are in the world." I Peter 5:8-9*

I would not say that we have a divine appointment with evil but rather we have an ongoing battle. God has given us all that is necessary to overcome. We just need to use what he has provided. We are led into the battle so we can defeat evil and live a victorious Christian life. (Check out my other book, "How To Live A Victorious Christian Life" at www.marinellichristianbooks.com)

Divine Appointments With Unsaved Folks

Not all divine appointments are with anointed Christians. God will bring you into the world of the unsaved so you can shine your light and testify to the saving grace of God through Jesus.

The Beggar

I remember a time when I was working at a men's clothing store in downtown Orlando. It was many years ago. As I left work and came to my car, a young man stopped me and asked for some money. I didn't have much to give but I remembered what Peter and John did when entering the temple in Jerusalem. They encounter a beggar seeking alms. Peter said, in so many words, "I don't have money but what I do have I will give you freely."

So I said the same thing to my beggar. However, all I had was a pocket size New Testament. I gave it to him, shared Christ with him and led him to a saving knowledge of Christ. Then he went on his way and so did I. However, I was rejoicing that another soul came into the kingdom of God. It truly was a divine appointment.

The Wood Chopper

There was a story I heard at a revival years ago that also illustrated divine appointments with unsaved folks. It was about an old woman that needed her wood chopped so she could use it to keep warm. Every day, she stood on her porch and prayed out loud, "Dear God, I need my wood chopped. Please help me"

As she prayed, an unsaved man came by, every day, and laughed at her because she prayed that God to send someone to chop her wood. He just shook his head as he passed by and mumbled to himself, "How silly"

About the third day, he stopped, picked up the ax and started chopping the old woman's wood. He complained all the time about how silly the old woman was. As he chopped the wood, the old woman praised God for meeting her need.

Now the moral of the story is…God will set up divine appointments for you to meet your need, even if the other person is ridiculing you. The Bible supports this notion. Proverbs 13:22b ... the wealth of the sinner is laid up for the just.

Divine Appointments With Godly Folks

It's no secret that God uses his children to bless each other. We are usually blessed in abundance so we have more than enough. That happens so we can be a blessing to others.

It's a good thing to have God on your side and orchestrating divine appointments on your behalf. He will give you favor with others as you seek to do His will.

We recently had a situation where a radiator hose split and coolant sprayed all over the engine. We were stranded away from any source of help. As we sat there wondering what to do, a man stopped and wanted to help. He took me up to an auto parts store where I bought the hose and then he installed it for me on the roadside. It so happened that a similar thing happened to him and a person stopped, bought him a battery and installed it so he could go on with his life. He said he was just being a good neighbor.

Divine Appointments With God

We cannot leave out divine appointments with God. The Old Testament tells the story of Job and his encounter with God. It also tells of the burning bush and Moses' divine encounter. The Bible is full of divine appointments where God and man met to discuss current or future events.

I remember a time, many years ago, when I was backslidden and away from God. I was praying that I might get back but just couldn't seem to overcome the darkness. Then one day, I hired a secretary that was a new, on fire, Christian. She later became my wife. However, she would often ask me why I was so mad at God.

One day, she came at me with the same questioning tone. But, instead of seeing her and hearing her, I saw into the Spirit and actually met with Jesus. I didn't physically see him, just felt his presence. There was an exchange of thought, no audible words, but I knew what he was saying.

He said to me, "It's a long way back, John. Do you want to make the trip?" By this time, I was in tears. I said, "Yes Lord" and he said, "Ok, walk with me and I will be at your side." Then his presence vanished but it left an impression on my heart that has never faded. This was 39 years ago and I am still rejoicing over that divine appointment with the Jesus.

Divine Appointments With Death

We all die. Sooner or later, we will pass on from this life into another. Where we spend eternity is our choice. The Bible tells us that even death is a divine appointment. "And as it is appointed unto men once to die, but after this the judgment:" Hebrews 9:27

Judgment will follow this divine appointment. We want to be sure that our days of judgment are nil. The way to eliminate God's wrath is to trust in Jesus. See what is said in the very next verse of Hebrews nine…verse 28… *"So Christ was once offered to bear the sins of many; and unto them that look for him shall he appear the second time without sin unto salvation"*

Jesus paid the debt owed to God's own Justice. It is paid in full so we, even though sinners, can go free. Now we can serve God and have fellowship with him without fear of death, hell or eternal judgment.

Holy Spirit Appointments

The question comes, how does a Christian have the Holy Spirit make such appointments for him? The answer is one word---YIELD! Every morning when you get up yield yourself to the Holy Spirit. Oh, how many opportunities he has for us if we would only be available to him and present ourselves for his use!

Notice the sensitivity of deacon Philip to this leadership in Acts 8:29, "Then the Spirit said unto Philip, Go near, and join thyself to this chariot." Notice, the Holy Spirit led him specifically to the eunuch's chariot! Then when the eunuch was won to Christ, Philip was caught away by the Spirit to another place. Verse 39, "And when they were come up out of the water, the Spirit of the Lord caught away Philip, that the eunuch saw him no more: and he went on his way rejoicing."

Divine Appointments And Evangelism

All believers are called to shine their lights into a dark or sinful world. We are instructed to go into the whole world and preach the gospel. This is one privilage we have…to share our faith. However, if you have encountered great resistance and feel that you are just not getting through to those around you that are not saved, here's a thought to consider.

Pray that the Holy Spirit will set up a divine appointment with that individual or group you are seeking to reach. Do not labor over it. Give it up to God to work it out. He is great enough to soften a heart, prepare the way, open the door and make it happen. Your job is to just be sensitive to the voice of the Spirit and wait for the appointment. Say nothing, just wait upon the Lord with an expectation that it will happen and be ready.

Selected Scriptures
Relative To Divine Appointments

1—Psalm 32:8..."I will instruct you and teach you in the way you should go; I will counsel you and watch over you."

2—Joshua 1:8..."Do not let this Book of the Law depart from your mouth; meditate on it day and night so that you may be careful to do everything written in it. Then you will be prosperous and successful."

3—Psalm 139:13–14a..."For you created my inmost being; you knit me together in my mother's womb. I praise you because I am fearfully and wonderfully made."

4—Ephesians 2:10..."For we are God's workmanship, create in Christ Jesus to do good works, which God prepared in advance for us to do."

5—1 Thessalonians 5:24..."The one who calls you is faithful and He will do it."

6—James 1:2–3..."Consider it pure joy, my brothers, whenever you face trials of many kinds, because you know that the testing of your faith develops perseverance."

7—2 Corinthians 5:7..."We walk by faith, not by sight."

8—Psalm 143:8..."Let the morning bring me word of your unfailing love, for I have put my trust in you. Show me the way I should go, for to you, I lift up my soul."

9—Colossians 3:2..."Set your minds on things above, not on earthly things."

10—Philippians 2:3–4..."Do nothing out of selfish ambition or vain conceit, but in humility consider others better than yourselves. Each of you should look not only to your own interest, but also to the interests of others."

11—Matthew 6:21..."For where your treasure is, there your heart will be also."

12—Philippians... 1:6..."Being confident of this, that he who began a good work in you will carry it on to completion until the day of Christ Jesus."

The Primary Reason For Divine Appointments

Hear what Jesus said to over 500 followers just before ascending into heaven. This was after his resurrection.

"And Jesus came and spake unto them, saying, all power is given unto me in heaven and in earth. Go ye therefore, and teach all nations, baptizing them in the name of the Father, and of the Son, and of the Holy Ghost: Teaching them to observe all things whatsoever I have commanded you: and, lo, I am with you always, even unto the end of the world. Matthew 28:18-20

We are commissioned to go and teach all nations. That can be your neighbor, your husband or wife, certainly kids and everyone else that enters your world. We just need to be sensitive to the leading of the Holy Spirit and ready at all times to share Christ. This is the primary reason for divine appointments.

Question? When was the last time you had a divine appointment? If you never had one, it's time. Here are a few things to consider that will ensure divine appointments on a regular basis.

1. Seek God's will, not your own.
2. Obey what you know to be true.
3. Read the scriptures and apply or walk in them.
4. Listen for the voice of the Holy Spirit.

5. Stand in faith and walk by faith.
6. Resist the devil, other folk's opinions and your own feelings.
7. Be prepared to share Christ at any time and in every situation.

CHAPTER ELEVEN

FINDING GOD'S WILL FOR YOUR LIFE

Now that you know the signs of the times leading up to the end and realize that evil is at your doorstep, it's time to decide which road you will walk towards the end of time. You can go with the crowd on the broad road that will lead to destruction or you can take the narrow path that leads to eternal life. However, the narrow path requires that you know God's will for your life. It is the only way to make it safely to the end of time and survive the experience.

When I was a young Christian, I didn't know God's will for my life. I wished with all my heart that I could actually know the will of God. I often sent up prayers to heaven saying, "Lord, what do I do now?" It got so bad that I could hardly drive my car because I couldn't decide if God wanted me in the left or right lane.

Months went by with my continual prayers to God as I shouted into heaven, "What Do I Do Now?" Finally, I was invited to a Bible study, started going to church and began reading my Bible. The answers came ever so slowly but fast enough for me to digest and store them away in my heart.

Now, after 60+ years of Bible study, prayer and life-application, I can say with confidence that I do know and understand "God's

Will" for me. I am still learning and studying and applying. I even, at times, ask my self, "Why didn't I see that before now?"

I am going to open your eyes if you are blind, refresh your spirit if it is weary and strengthen your personal walk with Jesus, our Savior, by providing the tools needed to keep you keeping on. *Hang on!* It's sure to be an exciting adventure.

Knowing That You Know

If you call yourself a Child of God, you should agree with me that you ought to know the Will of your Heavenly Father. You are openly admitting to a relationship and claiming family rights and access. **Are we in agreement so far?**

Knowing God is a logical assumption when we claim to be his child. Yet most of the Christians I know have serious doubts about the "Will of God" for them. This can only mean one of two things:

1. *Their relationship with God the Father is not a close one.* They pray, he listens, but they rarely feel his presence or hear his voice....*or*
2. *They have claimed to be a child of God but really are not.* They know there is something not right but are too ashamed or afraid to openly admit to not being a child of God.

In either case mentioned above, there is a way to *"know that you know"* so there is no more doubt. However, knowing that you know takes Faith. God is speaking all the time through the Bible, through his Spirit and through other folks that he brings into your life. The quick fix to *"Knowing That You Know"* is to *"Listen And Believe"*.

I can say, without a doubt, that I know the Will of God for my life. I can make such a claim because God, my Heavenly Father, has published 66 books that contain over 3,000 promises and many great statements as to what his will is for his children. It's all there in the Bible, just waiting for you to dig it out, *"Listen And Believe"*.

To know that you know is a great feeling because there is no anxiety in it. I know and have been persuaded that this way is the right way and my new perspective brings me a lot of comfort, peace and hope for the future.

"And thine ears shall hear a word behind thee, saying, this *is* the way, walk ye in it, when ye turn to the right hand, and when ye turn to the left." Isaiah 30:21

The Bible says, "For ye have not received the spirit of bondage again to fear; but ye have received the Spirit of adoption, whereby we cry, *Abba, Father*. The Spirit itself bears witness with our spirit, that we are the children of God: And if children, then heirs; heirs of God, and joint-heirs with Christ; if so be that we suffer with him, that we may be also glorified together." Romans 8:15-17

As the scripture says, the Spirit of God will bear witness with our spirits that we are the children of God. If you've ever felt, seen or otherwise realized the witness of God's Spirit, you will know without a shadow of a doubt, that you are a child of God.... and if a child also a joint heir with Christ.

How Does The Holy Spirit Bear Witness With Our Spirit?

Notice that the apostle Paul didn't say that the Spirit bears witness with our flesh, our souls or minds. He didn't say the witness would be through the intellect. He said the witness would be from *Spirit to spirit*. That means it could be one of many gentle quiet assurances that we did the right thing at the right time. It could be a sense of stability when things are going rough. It could be, an "I just know" feeling.

The point here is that God's Spirit is talking to us and our spirit is listening and rejoicing that it can hear God when he speaks. One definite witness, that I can recall, is when I read the scriptures, they started jumping off the page with new and fresh revelation. The Bible, all of a sudden, came alive and spoke directly to my spirit. God's Holy Spirit was and is still confirming to me that I am a child of the Living God.

So we have a quiet assurance and a loud voice that calls us to the Word of God, where we receive faith, instruction, assurance, strength, and knowledge and a lot more. God's witness is everywhere.

It's Not Rocket Science

Finding God's Will is not rocket science. We have already learned that God's Holy Spirit is available to confirm or excuse our decisions in life. We also know that it is our," Free Will" that engages truth and activates faith to empower us to walk in the Spirit.

The key to *"Knowing That You Know"* is absolute submission to his Will. Here's what Jesus said, "If any man will do his will, (God's Will), he shall know of the doctrine, whether it be of God, or whether I speak of myself." John 17:7

We have to be ready and willing to do his Will. When we are, we will know the doctrine or revelation knowledge necessary to accomplish the revealed Will of God.

Question! Why should God give us the knowledge of his Will if we are not willing or not ready to use it? That would be a waste of time and energy on God's part and he just doesn't operate that way.

He has, however, already revealed his Will in the pages of the Bible. If we really want to know, we can read and discover and learn and apply all that God has for us. So, let's look at the Bible?

I will take you on a journey so you can discover some of the great and precious promises that prove out what the Will of God is. We will look at several scriptures and discuss them.

God's Divine Will As Revealed In The Bible

"And God said, Let us make man in our image, after our likeness: and let them have dominion over the fish of the sea, and over the fowl of the air, and over the cattle, and over all the earth, and over every creeping thing that creeps upon the earth." Genesis 1:26

God wanted to create man, (Mankind or Male & Female). His divine will was to create us. He did that in his likeness and image. Then He gave us dominion over the earth and all its life forms. *What does this say to us?* Simply this, we were not a mistake, after thought or freak mutation of nature that evolved over millions of years. We were a specific, deliberate design to accomplish the goals and objectives of God in the earth.

"And let them have dominion." Genesis 1:26 The word, "Them" is all of us. We were to rule as the "Head" and not the Tail.

> *Now, let's proceed on our journey to discover the revealed "Will of God."*

Revelation #1...*God's will for our lives is to take dominion over evil and live in such a way as to reveal the image and likeness of God.*

Man Is Created Male & Female

Genesis 2:18-25 is the biblical record of God creating woman as a help meet for Adam. "And the LORD God said, It is not good that the man should be alone; I will make him a helper suitable for him."

"And the LORD God caused a deep sleep to fall upon Adam, and he slept: and he took one of his ribs, and closed up the flesh instead thereof; And the rib, which the LORD God had taken from man, made he a woman, and brought her unto the man. And Adam said, This *is* now bone of my bones, and flesh of my flesh: she shall be called Woman, because she was taken out of Man. Therefore shall a man leave his father and his mother, and shall cleave unto his wife: and they shall be one flesh. And they were both naked, the man and his wife, and were not ashamed."

Revelation #2... *It is God's Will for a man to have a woman at his side.* God ordained marriage and joined them together. Where does this leave Homosexuality? It was never in the will of God.

Revelation #3... *God's greatest creation, (Mankind), fell into sin and is now in need of a Savior.* The redemption of man was and is still God's will.

The Fall of Man
Death In Adam, Life In Christ

(Genesis 3:1-7; Genesis 7:1-5; 2 Peter 3:1-9)

I said this in earlier chapters but am restating it so you have the revelation now as well. "Wherefore, as by one man sin entered into the world, and death by sin; and so death passed upon all men, for that all have sinned: (For until the law sin was in the world: but sin is not imputed when there is no law. Nevertheless death reigned from Adam to Moses, even over them that had not sinned after the similitude of Adam's transgression, who is the figure of him that was to come." Romans 5:12-14

Romans 5:18-21 tells us, "Therefore as by the offence of one, *judgment came* upon all men to condemnation; even so by the righteousness of one, *the free gift came* upon all men unto justification of life. For as by one man's disobedience many were made sinners, so by the obedience of one, shall many be made righteous. Moreover the law entered, that the offence might abound. But where sin abounded, grace did much more abound: That as sin hath reigned unto death, even so might grace reign through righteousness unto eternal life by Jesus Christ our Lord."

Man falls from God's reality into the darkness of sin. He lost the image and likeness of God; But God still loves him and makes a plan for his restoration. Man Is justified by the blood of Jesus and His righteousness was imparted to us, that is, all who believe.

Revelation #4... *God loves us & does not want us to perish.* Jesus said, *"For God so loved the world, that he gave his only begotten Son, that whosoever believeth in him should not perish, but have everlasting life."* John 3:16 Whosoever believes is given eternal life.

"The Lord is not slack concerning his promise, as some men count slackness; but is longsuffering to us-ward, *not willing that any should perish, but that all should come to repentance."* II Peter 2:9 We must repent of our sin because Salvation is essential to knowing God's Will.

Revelation #5... *God wants us to repent and accept Jesus as our Savior so we can live in relationship with Him.*

"But God commended his love toward us, in that, while we were yet sinners, Christ died for us." Romans 5:8 He died for us that we might live for him. *(This is the foundation of the Gospel of Jesus Christ.)*

Revelation #6... *God wants us to live life with a thankful heart.* This allows God to be God over us and allows us to expresses our dependence upon him. It also relieves us from the burden and stress of being our own god. We don't have to be in control of everything.

Give Thanks In Everything

"In every thing give thanks: for this is the will of God in Christ Jesus concerning you." I Thessalonians 5:17

The Bible is filled with commands to give thanks to God (Psalm 106:1; 107:1; 118:1; 1 Chronicles 16:34; 1 Thessalonians 5:18). Most verses go on to list reasons why we should thank Him, such as "His love endures forever" (Psalm 136:3), "He is good" (Psalm 118:29), and "His mercy is everlasting" (Psalm 100:5). Thanksgiving and praise always go together. We cannot adequately praise and worship God without also being thankful.

Feeling and expressing appreciation is good for us. Like any wise father, God wants us to learn to be thankful for all the gifts He has given us (James 1:17). It is in our best interest to be reminded that everything we have is a gift from him. Without gratefulness, we become arrogant and self-centered. We begin to believe that we have achieved everything on our own. Thankfulness keeps our hearts in right relationship to God, the Giver of all good gifts.

Giving thanks also reminds us of how much we do have. Human beings are prone to covetousness. We tend to focus on what we *don't* have. By giving thanks continually we are reminded of how much we *do* have. When we focus on blessings rather than wants, we are happier. When we start thanking God for the things we usually take for granted, our perspective changes. We realize that we could not even exist without the merciful blessings of God." (Excerpts from www.gotquestions?org")

Revelation #7...*God is worthy of our trust and when we trust in, rely upon and adhere to his voice, he will direct our paths.*

Proverbs 3:5-6 offers another "Will of God" Revelation. *"Trust in the Lord with all thine heart; and lean not unto thine own understanding. In all thy ways acknowledge him, and he shall direct thy paths."*

Why should we trust the Lord? Many Christians ask that question because of adverse situations they are in or have gone through. Here are a few reasons:

1. **God is not a liar**. He will always deal with us from a vantage point of truth.
2. **God is immutable**, which means he can never change. He does not say one thing and do another. When He speaks... Well, listen to how Isaiah put it... *"So shall my word be that goes forth out of my mouth: it shall not return unto me void, but it shall accomplish that which I please, and it shall prosper in the thing whereto I sent it."* Isaiah 55:11
3. **God is Love...** This can only mean that he has no hate in him. His war and revenge is against his enemies who walk in darkness, steal, kill and destroy. His children are the *"Apple of His Eye"* and the subject of his grace.
4. **God is our Protector...**"The angel of the LORD encamps round about them that fear him, and delivers them." Psalm 34:7
5. **God really does care for us...**"Casting all your care upon him; for he cares for you." **I Peter 5:7** "Cast thy burden upon the LORD, and he shall sustain thee: he shall never suffer the righteous to be moved." Psalm 55:22
6. **God is a God of Blessings, Not Curses...**(Psalms 1:1-3) Blessed is the man who walks not in the counsel of the ungodly, nor stands in the path of sinners, nor sits in the seat of the scornful; {2} But his delight is in the law of the LORD, And in His law he meditates day and night. {3} He shall be like a tree planted by the rivers of water, that brings forth its fruit in its season, whose leaf also shall not wither; And whatever he does shall prosper.
7. **God is a God of Peace....** "And the God of peace shall bruise Satan under your feet shortly. The grace of our Lord Jesus Christ *be* with you. Amen." Romans 16:20

Because of who he is, we can, with confidence, acknowledge him, trust him, disregard our own feelings and follow his lead. He will always direct our paths.

Revelation #8...*God's highest will is to bring us back to where He had originally intended us to be, in His Image. Thus He speaks through the pages of the Bible, letting us know that He wants us to set ourselves apart for fellowship with Him.*

"For this is the will of God, even your sanctification, that ye should abstain from fornication:" I Thessalonians 4:3

The generic meaning of sanctification is "the state of proper functioning." To sanctify someone or something is to set that person or thing apart for the use intended by its designer. A pen is "sanctified" when used to write. Eyeglasses are "sanctified" when used to improve sight. In the theological sense, things are sanctified when they are used for the purpose God intends.

The Greek word translated "sanctification" (hagiasmos [aJgiasmov"]) means "holiness." To sanctify, therefore, means, "to make holy." In one sense only God is holy (Isa 6:3). God is separate, distinct, and there is no other. No human being or thing shares the holiness of God's essential nature. There is one God. Yet Scripture speaks about holy things. Moreover, God calls human beings to be "holyas" or holy as he is holy (Lev 11:44 ; Matt 5:48 ; 1 Peter 1:15-16). Another word for a holy person is "saint" (hagios [a&gio"]), meaning a sanctified one. The opposite of sanctified is "profane" (Lev 10:10).

The imperfect state of creation is a reminder that God's fully sanctified purpose for it has been disrupted by sin. Evil is the deprivation of the good that God intends for the creation He designed. The creation groans, awaiting its sanctification when everything will be set right (Rom 8:21-22 ; Rev. 20-21).

Human beings, made in God's image, were the pinnacle and focus of his creation. The sanctification of human beings, therefore, is the highest goal of God's work in the universe.

God explicitly declared it to be his will (1 Thess. 4:3). He purposed that human beings be "like him" in a way no other created thing is. Human beings are like God in their stewardship over creation (Gen 1:26-31). Yet this role is dependent on a more fundamentally important likeness to God-moral character. By virtue of God-given discretionary autonomy (faith), human beings may so depend upon God that his moral character (communicable attributes) are displayed. (Dictionaries - Baker's Evangelical Dictionary of Biblical Theology - Sanctification)

We can never be holy in ourselves as he is Holy but by faith, we can become the very righteousness of God in Jesus Christ. "For he (God) hath made him (Jesus) *to be* sin for us, who knew no sin; that we might be made the righteousness of God in him." II Corinthians 5:21

Revelation #9... *God wants us to allow the mind of Christ to be in us and to join Him in humility, and servitude so He can highly exalt us with Christ.*

"Let this mind be in you which was also in Christ Jesus, who, being in the form of God, did not consider it robbery to be equal with God, but made himself of no reputation, taking the form of a bondservant, and coming in the likeness of men. And being found in appearance as a man, he humbled himself and became obedient to the point of death, even the death of the cross. Therefore God also has highly exalted him and given him the name which is above every name, that at the name of Jesus every knee should bow, of those in heaven, and of those on earth, and of those under the earth, and that every tongue should confess that Jesus Christ is Lord, to the glory of God the Father." Philippians 2:5-11

Revelation #10...*God wants His Peace to Rule or referee in our hearts.*

"And let the peace of God rule in your hearts, to the which also ye are called in one body; and be ye thankful." Colossians 3:15

The word "Rule" in verse 15 actually expresses the intent to "Reign". It also can be interpreted as Referee as in a game. Paul is telling the church to allow the peace of God to referee any and all situations as though they were a game. By doing so, you can use God's peace as a referee's whistle. It will blow with anxiety, confusion, worry and so on to let you know that you are off sides and in need of a reconnect with the Holy Spirit to attain his peace and sustain an attitude of thankfulness.

If you find yourself in anger, worry or any other such attitude, you can automatically know that you have lost God's peace. God wants you to walk and live in his peace so you do not have to experience all that jazz of the flesh. It will kill you if left unattended.

Revelation #11...*God wants us to prove what is the good, and perfect will of God.*

"And be not conformed to this world: but be ye transformed by the renewing of your mind, that ye may prove what *is* that good, and acceptable, and perfect, will of God." Romans 12:1

We cannot allow non-believers to define what is or is not acceptable for the perfect Will of God. We need to be the Bible that they will not read. We need to demonstrate what good is and what perfect is so others around us can see what the perfect will of God is.

The only way to get the job done is to reject the pull of this world into all its sin and be transformed in our minds so we do not fall for the wiles of the devil. (Check out other Books at www.marinelichristianbooks.com)

How do we renew our minds? By transforming your own mind from always thinking evil to allowing the mind of Christ to dwell in you. He will do the rest. Your mission is to not be conformed to this world but to align yourself with God's Will.

Revelation #12… God wants us to Put on the whole armor of God so the devil can't hurt us.

"Finally, my brethren, be strong in the Lord, and in the power of his might. Put on the whole armor of God, that ye may be able to stand against the wiles of the devil. For we wrestle not against flesh and blood, but against principalities, against powers, against the rulers of the darkness of this world, against spiritual wickedness in high places. Wherefore take unto you the whole armor of God, that ye may be able to withstand in the evil day, and having done all, to stand." Ephesians 6:10-13

Our fight is with the rulers of darkness. We are fighting because we need to defend ourselves. If we don't, we will become open game for the devil. Hear again what Peter says in I Peter 5:8-9,

"Be sober, be vigilant; because your adversary the devil, as a roaring lion, walks about, seeking whom he may devour: Whom resist stedfast in the faith, knowing that the same afflictions are accomplished in your brethren that are in the world."

Revelation #13…*God Wants Us to Guard our Hearts With All Diligence.*

"Keep your heart with all diligence; for out of it are the issues of life." Proverbs 4:23 To keep ones heart is to guard it with all diligence. It implies that we should act as a gatekeeper that allows good things in and bad things from getting in. God wants us to protect our spiritual growth and resources. They can be depleted and even stolen by the devil.

Revelation #14…*God Wants Us to Pray Without Ceasing*

"Rejoice always, pray without ceasing, give thanks in all circumstances; for this is the will of God in Christ Jesus for you." I Thessalonians 5:16-18

We pray without ceasing when we start our day talking to God and maintain an atmosphere of prayer all day. We rejoice and give thanks along the way and life flows along like a calm gentle sea.

Revelation #15... God Wants Us To Have *Fellowship With Him.*

Fellowship With God

"That which was from the beginning, which we have heard, which we have seen with our eyes, which we have looked upon, and our hands have handled, of the Word of life;" I John 1:1

This simple and bold statement means that one can have a relationship with *God*. This idea would surprise many of John's readers, and it should be astounding to us. The Greek mind-set highly prized the idea of *fellowship*, but restricted to men among men - the idea of such an intimate relationship with God was revolutionary.

Jesus started the same kind of revolution among the Jews when he invited men to address God as *Father* (Matthew 6:9). We really can have a living, breathing relationship with God the Father, and with Jesus Christ. He can be, not only our Savior, but also our counselor and our closest friend.

Actually, for many people this is totally unappealing. Sometimes it is because they don't know who God is, and an invitation to a "personal relationship with God" is about as attractive to them as telling an eighth-grader they can have a "personal relationship with the assistant principal." But when we know the greatness, the goodness, and the glory of God, we *want* to have a relationship with him.

Other people turn from this relationship with God because they feel so distant from him. They *want* a relationship with God, but feel so disqualified, so distant. They need to know what God has done to make this kind of relationship possible.

The apostle John identified this eternally existent being, who was physically present with John and others as the Word of Life. This is the same *Logos* spoken of in John 1:1.

The idea of the *Logos* - of the Word - was important for John and for the Greek and Jewish worlds of his day. For the Jew, God was often referred to as *the Word* because they knew God perfectly revealed himself in his Word. For the Greek, their philosophers had spoken for centuries about the *Logos* - the basis for organization and intelligence in the universe, the Ultimate Reason that controls all things.

It is as if John said to everyone, "This *Logos* you have been talking about and writing about for centuries - well, we have heard him, seen him, studied him, and touched him. Let me now tell you about him."

This life was manifested, meaning that it was made actually and physically real. John testified as an eyewitness (we have seen, and bear witness, and declare to you) that this was the case. This was no fairy tale, no "Once upon a time" story. This was real, and John tells us about it as an eyewitness. (Excerpts from *David Guzik article on Fellowship With God*)

Revelation #16... *God Wants Us To Seek His Kingdom First, Above All Else In life.*

"But seek ye first the kingdom of God, and his righteousness; and all these things shall be added unto you." Matthew 6:33

Jesus said to seek first the <u>kingdom of God</u> in his Sermon on the

Mount (Matthew 6:33). The verse's meaning is as direct as it sounds. We are to seek the things of God as a priority over the things of the world. Primarily, it means we are to seek the salvation that is inherent in the kingdom of God because it is of greater value than all the world's riches.

Does this mean that we should neglect the reasonable and daily duties that help sustain our lives? Certainly not. But for the Christian, there should be a difference in attitude toward them. If we are taking care of God's business as a priority—seeking his salvation, living in obedience to him, and sharing the good news of the kingdom with others—then he will take care of our business as he promised—and if that's the arrangement, where is worrying?

But how do we know if we're truly seeking God's kingdom first? There are questions we can ask ourselves. "Where do I primarily spend my energies? Is all my time and money spent on goods and activities that will certainly perish, or in the services of God—the results of which live on for eternity?" Believers who have learned to truly put God first may then rest in this holy dynamic: "…and all these things will be given to you as well."

God has promised to provide for his own, supplying every need (Philippians 4:19), but His idea of what we need is often different from ours, and his timing will only occasionally meet our expectations.

A growing number of false teachers are gathering followers under the message "God wants you to be rich!" But that philosophy is not the counsel of the Bible. It is certainly not the counsel of Matthew 6:33, which is not a formula for gaining wealth. It is a description of how God works. Jesus taught that our focus should be away from this world—its status and its lying allurements—and placed upon the things of God's kingdom. (Excerpts from gotquestions?org)

Matthew 6:33 is a call to priorities. We are invited to have fellowship with Christ but not in the appetites of sinful flesh. He wants us to walk with him in his kingdom. Jesus says that if we sell out to him, he will provide for us but if our selling out is to get rich, we have missed it before we start. God certainly wants us to prosper and be in good health but not by manipulation or exultation of self.

Revelation #17... *God wants us to be filled with His Holy Spirit*

"And be not drunk with wine, wherein is excess; but be filled with the Spirit; Speaking to yourselves in psalms and hymns and spiritual songs, singing and making melody in your heart to the Lord;" Ephesians 5:18-19

This scripture clearly reveals God's Will for his followers: Don't get drunk, Be Filled and Sing. I want to focus more closely on being filled with the Spirit. I am sure you will agree that he is not referring to the spirit of evil or the human spirit of which we are already absorbed. It is obvious that the Spirit we need to be filled with is none other than the Spirit of The Lord.

How does one get filled with God's Spirit? The text here uses Greek words that mean to be continually filled as though it were possible to use up the Spirit and find yourself to be empty. I think that many Christians are running on empty and are in serious need of a fill-up.

Paul wrote: "Do not get drunk on wine, which leads to debauchery. Instead, be filled with the Spirit." In the original Greek, the phrase "be filled: is a present-tense verb.

To signify a "one-time filling," Paul would have used the past tense or a future verb tense; instead, he chose the present tense to denote that the filling of the Holy Spirit is not a one-time event, but a continual experience. Scripture says that we must be continually filled with the Spirit, not just once or twice.

The word filling seems awkward when referring to the Holy Spirit's entrance into our lives. The Spirit of God is not a liquid, like water. He does not fill a person the way cold milk fills a cup. The Holy Spirit is God—He is one in essence with the Father and the Son—but he is also a distinct personality and has all the attributes thereof. That is why we refer to the Holy Spirit as the third person of the Trinity. Many Scripture passages point to these facts.

Like a person, the Holy Spirit searches, helps and guides. He knows; He feels; He wills. Scripture speaks of the Holy Spirit's mind, His love and his instruction. In Ephesians 4:30, Paul wrote: "Do not grieve the Holy Spirit of God, with whom you were sealed for the day of redemption." The only way we can grieve someone is if the one we are grieving has feelings.

Because the Holy Spirit is a personality, it makes more sense to talk about the Holy Spirit's control or compulsion in our lives, rather than his filling of our lives. Holy Spirit-driven is a good way to look at our response to His control.

A person who is filled with the Spirit is driven by the Spirit—driven in a gentle, loving way. A Spirit-driven person allows the Holy Spirit to direct and guide every decision. Because the world, the flesh and the devil oppose the Spirit-controlled lifestyle, we need to be filled and renewed continually. (Excerpts taken from Joel Comiskey's article CBN.org.)

Baptism with the Holy Spirit or in the Holy Spirit in Christian theology is a term describing baptism (washing or immersion) in or with the Spirit of God and is frequently associated with the bestowal of spiritual gifts and empowerment for Christian ministry. (Acts 1:5,8)

To illustrate, consider this…if we drank water from a glass, then the water would be inside us. However, if we went to the beach and stepped into the ocean, then we would be in the water. We receive, as it were, a drink of the Holy Spirit when we are saved, but when we are baptized in the Spirit, it is as if that initial drink becomes an ocean that completely surrounds us.

Just as the indwelling Spirit that Christians receive when they are saved reproduces *the life* of Jesus, so the outpoured, or baptizing, Spirit reproduces *the ministry* of Jesus, including miracles and healings.

When Jesus gave the Great Commission (Matthew 28:19-20), He knew that His disciples could not fulfill it in their own power. Therefore, He had a special gift in store for them: It was His plan to give them the same power that he had -- the power of the Spirit of God. So, immediately after giving them the Great Commission, Jesus commanded his disciples not to leave Jerusalem, but to wait for what the Father promised, "which," he said, "you heard of from Me; for John baptized with water, but you shall be baptized with the Holy Spirit not many days from now" (Acts 1:4-5). He further promised: "You shall receive power when the Holy Spirit has come upon you; and you shall be my witnesses both in Jerusalem, and in all Judea and Samaria, and even to the remotest part of the earth" (Acts 1:8).

The disciples waited in Jerusalem as Jesus had commanded, and one day when they were all together, "suddenly there came from heaven a noise like a violent, rushing wind, and it filled the whole house where they were sitting. And there appeared to them tongues as of fire distributing themselves, and they rested on each one of them. And they were filled with the Holy Spirit and began to speak with other tongues, as the Spirit was giving them utterance" *(Acts 2:3,4)*. Then Peter explained to the crowd that gathered that they were seeing the working of God's Spirit and told them about Jesus. The Christian church began that day with the disciples and the three thousand people who joined them as a result of the day's events.

We can undertake making disciples of all nations with some degree of success without the baptism in the Holy Spirit, but when we do, we are undertaking a supernatural task with limited power.

It is God's will -- it is His commandment -- that we be baptized with and continually filled with the Holy Spirit: *"Be filled with the Spirit"* (Ephesians 5:18). The knowledge and reality of the empowering Spirit enables us to reproduce the works of Jesus. (Excerpts from CBN.org)

So, as I see it, the baptism of the Spirit is given so the believer can receive ministry gifts to aid in his or her service to the lord. The In-filling of the Spirit is to replenish the refreshing required to continue day to day. One has to do with reaching out to others. The other has to do with hearing and fellowshipping with God so we have direction, purpose and a clear focus.

Revelation #18... *God Wants Us to Know That He Is Working Everything Together For Good.*

Why should we Trust God, Give Thanks, Pray Without Ceasing, and follow all the other teachings of Jesus? I would venture to say because of Romans 8:28 ," And we know that all things work together for good to them that love God, to them who are the called according to his purpose."

God's Will is clearly revealed but only accomplished in the lives of those that Love God and are the called according to his purposes. We also know that God calls everyone to repentance and salvation (John 3:16) The next pre-qualifier is that we love God. You would think that his children love their father. If they do not, it's because they do not know him. In any event, Loving God is the prime directive. Jesus said, "And thou shalt love the Lord thy God with all thy heart, and with all thy soul, and with all thy mind, and with all thy strength: this is the first commandment." Mark 12:30

I am sure you will see even more scriptures that will reveal the "Will of God" for your life as you keep reading the Bible. I have listed some more prominent ones so you can get a feel for what to look for as you read.

So far we have discovered 18 that should be active in our lives today. These revelation truths are as follows:

- *God's will for our lives is to take dominion over evil and live in such a way as to reveal the image and likeness of God.*
- *It is God's Will for a man to have a woman at his side.*
- *God's greatest creation, (Mankind), fell into sin and is now in need of a Savior.*
- *God loves us & does not want us to perish.*
- *God wants us to repent and accept Jesus as our Savior so we can live in relationship with Him.*
- *God wants us to live life with a thankful heart.*
- *God is worthy of our trust and when we trust in, rely upon and adhere to His voice, He will direct our paths.*
- *God's highest will is to bring us back to where He had originally intended us to be, in His Image. Thus He speaks through the pages of the Bible, letting us know that He wants us to set ourselves apart for fellowship with Him.*
- *God wants us to allow the mind of Christ to be in us and to join Him in humility, and servitude so He can highly exalt us with Christ.*
- *God wants His Peace to Rule or referee in our hearts.*
- *God wants us to prove what is the good, and perfect will of God.*
- *God wants us to Put on the whole armor of God so the devil can't hurt us.*

- God Wants Us to Gu*ard our Hearts With All Diligence.*
- God Wants Us to *Pray Without Ceasing*
- God Wants Us To Have *Fellowship With Him.*
- God Wants Us To Seek His Kingdom First, Above All Else In life.
- *God wants us to be filled with His Holy Spirit*
- *God Wants Us to Know That He Is Working Everything Together For Good.*

The best way to find God's Will for your life is not to ask friends, family, or anyone else. They are not God and often are wrong in their own decisions, which, if I am right, will show up in their lives as a testimony against them.

The best way to know God's Will is to ask God in prayer, stay in the Bible and look for direction, correction and guidance. ***It's all there.*** If you start a log of scripture verses and what they specifically meant to you, you'll have a history to refer to when you feel lost or confused.

<u>Remember This</u>

All scripture *is* given by inspiration of God, and *is* profitable for doctrine, for reproof, for correction, for instruction in righteousness:

II Timothy 3:16

The Best way to live in this world is to apply the scriptures and live in them moment by moment. The truth you find in the scriptures will far exceed what this world has to offer.

CHAPTER TWELVE

THE RAPTURE OF THE CHURCH

IT IS MY BELIEF THAT the end of the world for a believer in Christ is an eithor/or situation. I say either because our world ends when we die. I speak of life on earth. It is over, at least until we rise from the grave at the rapture. However, our hope is that we will live to see the Lord descending from heaven to gather up his church which we are. So in the either or the "or" scenario, we will be with the Lord.

Some Opinions As To Jesus' Return

Folks have predicted the exact day when Jesus will return but over the years those exact days came and went and he did not show up. I guess he didn't get the memo. We are still waiting and some folks are saying lots of different things. Here are some that I have heard:

1. He is supposed to come for a glorious church, without spot or wrinkle and the church has not evolved to that point yet.
2. All the signs are not as yet revealed so He is waiting for those final signs.
3. Jesus' return has already happened and we missed it because it happened before we were born.
4. Jesus' return happened on the Day of Penticost and the church is supposed to now take charge and rule the world.
5. His return was never meant to be a single event but an on-go-

ing event from heart to heart of those that repent and become, "Born Again"

I am sure you have heard several that I did not list. The fact is, we are still waiting. That reminds me of a parable that Jesus taught to his disciples. It's found in Matthew 25:1-13.

"Then the kingdom of heaven will be like ten virgins who took their lamps and went to meet the bridegroom. Five of them were foolish, and five were wise, for when the foolish took their lamps, they took no oil with them, but the wise took flasks of oil with their lamps. As the bridegroom was delayed, they all became drowsy and slept. But at midnight there was a cry, 'Here is the bridegroom! Come out to meet him.' Then all those virgins rose and trimmed their lamps. And the foolish said to the wise, 'Give us some of your oil, for our lamps are going out. But the wise answered, saying, 'since there will not be enough for us and for you, go rather to the dealers and buy for yourselves. And while they were going to buy, the bridegroom came, and those who were ready went in with him to the marriage feast, and the door was shut. Afterward the other virgins came also, saying, "Lord, Lord, open to us." But he answered, "Truly, I say to you, I do not know you." Watch therefore, for you know neither the day nor the hour.

Here's what James Montgomery Boice wrote about this parable. He is a contributor for Logos Bible Software.... *As we take a good look at the Parable of the Ten Virgins (Matthew 25:1-13), we must acknowledge up front that there has been much debate as to the meaning of these words of our Savior.*

At least one aspect of this parable can be known with absolute certainty. The bridegroom is Jesus Christ, and this parable describes his return. Both the Old Testament (Isaiah 54:4-6; 62:4-5; Hosea 2:19) and the New Testament (John 3:27-30; Matthew 9:15; Mark 2:19-20) represent the Messiah as a bridegroom. The Church is described in scripture as the bride. (Ephesians 5:25-32)

The overall and easily seen thrust of the parable is that Christ will return at an unknown hour and that his people must be ready.

Being ready means preparing for whatever contingency arises in our lives and keeping our eyes fixed on Jesus at all times while we eagerly await his coming."

B. L. Cocherell and Charles E. Barrett of Biblesearch.org offer this interpretation:

"It is very clear that the ten virgins represent a significant part of the entire body of elect. Because of the warning messages in Revelation 2 and 3 to the seven churches of God which will exist just before Christ's return, it appears likely that the ten virgins represent all the elect that exist during the end of the age, except for those of the Philadelphia church.

Perhaps the reason that there are ten virgins divided into two groups is the numerical meaning of the numbers 10 and 5 as they apply to biblical symbolism. The number 10 is symbolic of the law of God and the number 5 is symbolic of God's grace.

This parable indicates that all of these people knew that the banquet would occur very soon and they were looking forward to the arrival of the bridegroom and participating in the celebration after his arrival."

The Wise And The Foolish

"Five of them were foolish and five were wise. The foolish ones took their lamps but did not take enough oil with them. The wise, however, took oil in jars along with their lamps" (Matthew 25:2-4).

Notice that Jesus separates the 10-vergins into two groups, the wise and the foolish. Both are waiting for his return. All of the virgins began with full lamps. It is obvious that all of the virgins were anticipating a period of waiting but none of them know just how long. All of them also identified themselves as the bride. They knew that there was a wedding banquet in their future. The wise anticipated that they might have to wait longer than expected so they brought extra oil in order to keep their lights burning as long as necessary.

The burning lamp is a picture of the Word of God. Psalm 119:105 verifies this, "Thy word is a lamp unto my feet, and a light unto my path." It is important to understand the symbolism of the lamps.

The lamp represents the principles upon which one's life is established. It is the Will of God given to man to guide him in the way of righteous and away from the snares of the devil. The Word of God symbolized by a lighted Lamp is the key to understanding this parable.

The emphasis seems to be on the importance of keeping one's lamp lit. *That is to say*, being so full of God's word that you shine like a beacon atop a hill overlooking the city. Didn't Jesus say, "Let your light so shine before men, that they may see your good works, and glorify your Father which is in heaven." Matthew 5:16

What happens when your light goes out? You guessed it; you fall into darkness where confusion, depression, sorrows and death dwell. The lamp that lit the way is out. The path is lost and you wander in the wilderness like the children of Israel of old. This is a picture of the 5-fooloish virgins and their ultimate destiny.

10 Virgins Equals Six Churches

I believe that the 10 virgins represent the six churches in Revelation that Jesus rebuked, it is also important to see that they all fell asleep. Only the 7th church, Philadelphia, stayed awake.

Here is the account in Revelation 17:7-9. It is a picture of the wife of the Lamb, which before being the wife was, as the parable teaches, 10 virgins waiting for the Bridegroom to come.

"Let us be glad and rejoice, and give honor to him: for the marriage of the Lamb is come, and his wife hath made herself ready. And to her was granted that she should be arrayed in fine linen, clean and white: for the fine linen is the righteousness of saints. And he saith unto me, Write, Blessed are they, which are called unto the marriage supper of the Lamb. And he saith unto me, these are the true sayings of God."

Who was called to the marriage supper of the Lamb? The 10 virgins and the church of Philadelphia are they that were called. They represent the Bride who became the wife.

To fall asleep, in my opinion, and others I read after, is to fall away from the truth. It's like forgetting that Jesus is really coming back and falling back into life as usual, like the world system of things. The zeal and dedication fades away and is eventually replaced with religion, rules, dogma and political correctness, the result of which is liberalism.

Nowhere in the message to the elect of Philadelphia, do we find them pictured as being asleep. On the contrary, they are shown as being the zealous elect who are commended for faithfully keeping the truth of God and upholding the name of Jesus.

Thus, it is clear that the parable of the 10 virgins is talking about the rest of the elect who are all spiritually asleep just before Christ's return. History shows us that because of spiritual lethargy the early church disappeared as a united, powerful entity. However, throughout the centuries, there have been a few among the elect of God who have kept awake while the great majority has gone to sleep. G. L. Cocherell and Charles E. Barrett

Today's Christian Community

If we are really in the last days before the return of Christ, which I believe we are, this parable is a clear picture of our Christian community. Do you know how many denominations there are in our modern world? According to the *Center for the Study of Global*

Christianity at Gordon-Conwell Theological Seminary, there were an estimated 34,000 denominations in 2000, rising to an estimated 43,000 in 2012. These numbers have exploded from 1,600 in the year 1900. Do you suppose that this is a picture of division, confusion and apathy? I do not see unity and brotherhood. I see virgins asleep (preoccupied with the cares of this world) I also see churches that have embraced immorality.

I was curious to see if I could find denominations that have affirmed the LBTG lifestyle. LBTG refers to Lesbian, Bisexual, Transgender and Gay. Here's what I found in a Google search. These denominations affirm the LBTG lifestyle:

Catholic, Baptist, Pentecostal, United Church of Christ, United Methodist, Brethren Mennonite, Presbyterian, Evangelical Anglican, Disciples of Christ, Independent Orthodox Greek, Lutheran, and Charismatic.

I realize that most of these denominations have many different offshoots and the above list does not necessarily portray full acceptance by the entire denomination mentioned. It does however; illustrate a trend towards immorality and worldly political correctness. It also shows a church that was once vibrant and on fire for God as falling asleep.

The majority of today's church felt that Christ's return was very near and would happen before the end of the century. Many people thought that he would return before 1975. We know that it didn't happen. The Philadelphia church went on in faith and stayed awake but the rest conveniently went to sleep. In other words, they believed that "The Lord delayed his coming" (Luke.12:45).

It should be noted that the Philadelphia church is scattered among every denomination. They are the believers that walk by faith and trust in the Lord. They are those that look for his coming and seek to live within the known will of God. They are those that hide his word in their hearts and fill themselves with his Spirit daily. They hear his voice and come to his calling. The return of Christ will be no surprise to them. They will be ready.

The Midnight Cry

"At midnight the cry rang out: 'Here's the bridegroom! Come out to meet him" Matthew 25:6. I believe that the cry at midnight comes from the church that did not fall asleep…the spiritual church that flows through most every denomination. They are watching and praying for his return and will, through the Spirit, sense his coming ahead of time.

"This cry of warning follows the pattern of all the warnings given by prophets to God's people throughout history. God never lets his people go into severe trials without a resounding warning and an opportunity to repent. The issue here is a very serious one. It is an issue of salvation or the Lake of Fire. This is not a minor reprimand or chastisement.

This is an issue of whether one will respond to the warning, repent, and return to the faith once delivered and return to God the Father and Jesus Christ in a proper attitude. The window of opportunity for true repentance seems very short. It appears likely that there will be little time to get one's spiritual house in order before the door to salvation is shut forever." *G. L. Cocherell and Charles E. Barrett*

This brings up a question about the salvation of those that ran out of oil. (the Word of God) All of the Virgins hear the cry. They all woke up. They all realized the seriousness of the cry. Everyone gets a wake up call but half didn't have any oil, Word of God. They are left behind. The Bridegroom comes and receives the wise virgins and shuts the door. The foolish virgins are denied access and hear the Lord say to them as they try to gain access, *"I don't know you."*

These foolish virgins did not take the Word, oil with them. They allowed the Word of God to slip away. They did not keep the truth of God alive in their hearts. They stopped walking by faith. In fact, they cut off the very source by which they could receive faith, the scriptures.

Is this a loss of one salvation? I think not. Hear what the scripture says.

"They went out from us, but they were not of us; for if they had been of us, they would *no doubt* have continued with us: but *they went out*, that they might be made manifest that they were not all of us." I John 2:19

" A sower went out to sow. And as he sowed, some seeds fell on the path, and the birds came and ate them up. Other seeds fell on rocky ground, where they did not have much soil, and they sprang up quickly, since they had no depth of soil. But when the sun rose, they were scorched; and since they had no root, they withered away. Other seeds fell among thorns, and the thorns grew up and choked them. Other seeds fell on good soil and brought forth grain, some a hundredfold, some sixty, some thirty. Let anyone with ears listen!" (Matthew 13:3-9).

"Another parable he put forth to them, saying: "The kingdom of heaven is like a man who sowed good seed in his field; but while men slept, his enemy came and sowed tares among the wheat and went his way. But when the grain had sprouted and produced a crop, then the tares also appeared. So the servants of the owner came and said to him, 'Sir, did you not sow good seed in your field? How then does it have tares?' He said to them, 'An enemy has done this.' The servants said to him, 'Do you want us then to go and gather them up?' But he said, 'No, lest while you gather up the tares you also uproot the wheat with them. Let both grow together until the harvest, and at the time of harvest I will say to the reapers, "First gather together the tares and bind them in bundles to burn them, but gather the wheat into my barn." Matthew 13:24-30

Here's what these three scriptures tell me: 1.) Some of our group is not really what they claim to be. 2.) Some of the folks that received the Word that was sown in their hearts by the sewer did not take it seriously and it did not take root. 3.) Some of the harvest is not really wheat at all but tares (weeds) fighting for the same ground.

The five foolish virgins, in my opinion, are really tares that sought to dominate the wheat. They used the oil or Word of God as a cover to hide their true identity but failed in the end to actually apply the scripture. They appeared to be with us but really were not. They could not make the transition from unrighteousness to righteousness. They ignored God's truth and ran out of oil, that is to say, the Word had no affect on them because it was not mixed with faith. In doing so, they have, in fact, sentenced themselves to the Lake of Fire.

Too Late Is Too Late

"And the door was shut. Later the others also came. Sir! Sir! they said, open the door for us! But he replied, I tell you the truth, I don't know you. Therefore keep watch, because you do not know the day or the hour wherein the Son of man comes" (Matthew 25:10-13).

The parable teaches that once the door is closed, it's just too late. The foolish virgins are excluded from the Marriage Supper of The Lamb because they were not really qualified or "Born Again".

Once the church is gathered from the earth, there will no longer be a person alive on earth that has the Spirit of God within them. This is documented in II Thessalonians 2:7, "For the mystery of iniquity doth already work: only he who now letteth will let, until he be taken out of the way."

I say it again…He that letteth, (or restrains), is the Holy Spirit. When he is taken out of the way, he has to take us with him because Jesus said, "And I will pray the Father, and he shall give you another Comforter, that he may abide with you for ever" John 14:16 This is why Jesus says to the foolish virgins, "I don't know you." They no longer have the Spirit of God available to them and they have lost their opportunity for salvation, which means that their fate is the Lake of Fire, because they were called of God but they did not repent and become, "Born Again". "The Lord is not slack concerning his promise, as some men count slackness; but is longsuffering to us-ward, not willing that any should perish, but that all should come to repentance." II Peter 3:9

Knowing How To Wait

As we Christians wait for our Lord's return, what should we be doing? This seems to be the best-kept secret ever. The devil just doesn't want us to know how to wait. He wants us to fall asleep which means to drift off center and leave our faith on the table. He wants us to follow our fleshly appetites and become one with the world system.

If we do this, we will show God and those around us that we were never really a Christian. We will show them that we are playing church and using what little scripture we know as a cloak to hide our inward unsaved condition. Eventually we will find one of the six churches that have fallen asleep and sleep there until the midnight call. That will be a day of reckoning. On the other hand, if we stay awake, we will be joining the Philadelphia church that walks by faith, prays for revelation and eagerly looks for his return.

There is a theological assumption in all of this. It is called, *"The Perseverance of The Saints"*. The premise is that true saints will not give up. They will instead persevere to the very end. If any give up, it is because he or she is not really a saint. This is not to say that saints do not stumble and fall. It is to say that when they do, they get back up and go on with their relationship with God.

Those that don't get up but give up and return to the world system. They are those that have no oil. They claim to be a saint but never had the, "Born Again" experience. I can see them now in the sleeping churches. They lack spiritual knowledge, know nothing of spiritual warfare, walk in the flesh instead of the Spirit and believe they can get to heaven through good works.

Signs of His Coming

Jesus said that when you see certain things begin to happen, *"Look up and lift up your heads, for your redemption draws near,"* and *"when you see them happen the kingdom of God is near."* (Luke 21:28,31)

Jesus and Paul both taught that the proper way to wait for his return is to therefore be *Watchful, Ready and Sober* (Matthew 24:42-44,25:13; 1 Th. 5:6).

Just to be sure, I present the signs of Jesus' coming and the end of the world. I say end of the world because Jesus will end it as we know it when he comes.

Wars And Rumors of Wars

"And you will hear of wars and rumors of wars. See that you are not troubled; for all these things must come to pass, but the end is not yet. For nation will rise against nation, and kingdom against kingdom." (Matthew 24:6,7a)

Since World War II, many countries have been building up massive arsenals of conventional and nuclear weapons. The potential for war grows day by day. In addition to potential nuclear war, we have war on terror, water wars, weather wars, and a host of various types that need not be named.

Famines, Pestilence, Earthquakes

"And there will be famines, pestilences, and earthquakes in various places. All these are the beginning of sorrows." (Matthew 24:7b,8). Due to flooding and droughts, world food supplies are running very low. Many people are expecting a global food shortage and famines.

Regarding earthquakes, scientific data does show that we have been seeing a large increase in seismic activity. According to a number of scientists, another star or large planet is affecting the sun's magnetic field, which is also affecting the earth's magnetic field - both the core and the ionosphere. The north pole is shifting at an accelerated pace, and the earth seems to be expanding. Thus, we should see a continual increase in earthquakes and volcanic activity in coming years.

Deceivers Who Claim To Be Christian

And Jesus answered and said to them: *"Take heed that no one deceives you for many will come in My name saying that I am the Christ and will deceive many."* Mt. 24:4,5

Although the Bible teaches that Jesus is the promised Jewish Messiah and is "the only begotten Son of God" (John 3:18), who created the world and everything in it (Col. 1:16), at the end of the church age many people will be teaching these truths, yet they will have other teachings that are not consistent with the Bible and will deceive many. Perhaps the majority of professing Christian teachers in the world today fall into this camp, as most have fallen away from sound Biblical teachings and instead place traditions of men and/or the goal of increasing church attendance above the authority of the Bible. Some are subtle, and some are blatant. Sincere followers of Jesus should come out of these wayward institutional churches and seek to fellowship with people who follow and teach what Jesus and his apostles did.

People of Israel Return To Their Land

"Behold, the days come, saith the LORD, that ... I will bring again captivity of my people of Israel, and they shall build the waste cities, and inhabit them; and they shall plant vineyards, and drink the wine thereof; they shall also make gardens, and eat the fruit of them. And I will plant them upon their land, and they shall no more be pulled up out of their land which I have given them, saith the LORD thy God." (Amos 9:13-15)

"Thus says the Lord GOD: 'Surely I will take the children of Israel from among the nations, wherever they have gone, and will gather them from every side and bring them into their own land; and I will make them one nation in the land, on the mountains of Israel." (Ezekiel 37:21,22)

During the last 130 years, Jews from 108 nations have migrated to the land of Israel.

In 1882 the first wave of modern immigration to Israel started as Jews fled persecution, or followed the Socialist Zionist ideas of Moses Hess. From 1882 to 1919 around 75,000 Jews immigrated to Palestine, mostly from Russia. They bought land from the Ottoman Empire and individual Arab landholders and established agricultural settlements. During this period the Hebrews language was revived, newspapers and literature were published in Hebrew and political parties and workers organizations were established.

In 1917 during World War I, the British government in its Balfour Declaration supported plans for a national home for the Jews in their promised land. Later, the Ottoman Empire (Turkey) lost control of the Middle East. This made it possible for hundreds of thousands more immigrants to arrive from Europe. Anti-Semitism drove most there. Many more would have come had it not been for Arab protest and resulting British restrictions on immigration.

Today, Israel's population is over 7 million. In 2018, Israel celebrated its 70th anniversary, but some of its neighbors hate it and want to "wipe it off the map". It is still mostly a secular state, but it has a growing percentage of Orthodox Jews and Christians. Today, the Aliyah immigration movement continues to embrace Jewish newcomers, to help them become a part of communities and help them learn Hebrew.

Increased Wickedness & Loss of Love

"And because lawlessness will abound, the love of many will grow cold." (Matthew 24:12)

Today, more and more people are living primarily for themselves and their own happiness. The idea of denying themselves, taking up their crosses daily and following Jesus (Luke 9:23) is a foreign concept. What TV and movies show as "normal" has affected the values of those who indulge in them. At the same time, couples are divorcing, and children are growing up with deep unmet needs. Many couples are not even marrying but living together in fornication (any form of sex not sanctioned by God). The result has been the blood sacrifice (murder) of millions of innocent, helpless unborn children through abortion, over 60 million in the United States alone and the birthing of even more children who lack a healthy home where they can receive love and training from their own father and mother.

Business As Usual

Jesus said, *"As it was in the days of Noah, so shall it be also in the days of the Son of man.* For as in those days before the flood they were eating and drinking, marrying and giving in marriage, until the day when Noah entered the ark, and they were unaware until the flood came and swept them all away, so will be the coming of the Son of Man" (Matthew 24:37-39). Note that the flood was unexpected. They were all unaware of its coming and its affect on them until it was too late. Noah was a preacher of righteousness who warned the people around him but no one listened.

Today, we have radio, T.V. and other media and we use it to tell folks that Jesus is coming soon but no one is really listening. The world is carring on with business as usual and will until it is just too late.

Strong Delusion

And for this reason God will send them strong delusion, that they should believe the lie. (2 Th. 2:11 NKJV)

The primary focus of the deception is the use of the controlled corporate media by the Prince of the Power of the Air. TV, radio, Internet, cell phones, etc. keep people completely preoccupied and oblivious to the fate that awaits them. The goal is also to prevent people from hearing the Gospel of Jesus, and if they do hear it to forget about it and be entertained constantly. Most people in developed countries are now in a fog due to the impact of these media that lulls them into a false sense of security and into a false sense of right and wrong. This delusion can be seen in three areas:

Spirituality... the Emerging Church has become so pervasive that most churches in developed countries will tolerate abortion (murder), fornication (premarital sex, adultery, homosexuality) and almost any other violation of God's law. Just think: how many churches will excommunicate a person for involvement in these sins?

Politics... most people are also unaware of the liberal media and left-wing parties that push their socialistic views and seek to change the very foundation by which our country was established. This political premise has called evil good and makes laws that protect imoral behavoir and the killing of unborn babies. They, the people, think it's ok. Their spiritual darkness is now called light that will guide our country into the future.

Let no one deceive you by any means; for that Day will not come unless the falling away comes first, and the man of sin is revealed, the son of perdition, who opposes and exalts himself above all that is called God or that is worshiped, so that he sits as God in the temple of God, showing himself that he is God. The coming of the lawless one is according to the working of Satan, with all power, signs, and lying wonders, and with all unrighteous deception among those who perish, because they did not receive the love of the truth, that they might be saved. And for this reason God will send them strong delusion, that they should believe the lie, that they all may be condemned who did not believe the truth but had pleasure in unrighteousness. (2 Thessalonians 2:3,4,9-12)

When Will Jesus Return?

Would you believe me if I told you that Jesus will return on the 3rd Friday of next month? Some have actually tried to predict the actual day of his return. I guess they never read the scripture that says, "But of that day and hour knoweth no *man*, no, not the angels of heaven, but my Father only." Matthew 24:36

Knowing the actual day or hour is impossible. Only God, the Father knows. However, we do know that it will be an unexpected event in the eyes of the world. "For yourselves know perfectly that the day of the Lord so cometh as a thief in the night". I Thessalonians 5:2

Why Is He Coming Back?

Jesus is coming back because he said he would. He is coming for us, the "Born Again" saints. "That he might present it to himself a glorious church, not having spot, or wrinkle, or any such thing; but that it should be holy and without blemish." Ephesians 5:27

Why Did He Go Away?

"In my Father's house are many mansions: if it were not so, I would have told you. I go to prepare a place for you. And if I go and prepare a place for you, I will come again, and receive you unto myself; that where I am, there ye may be also.' **John 14:2-3**

Jesus is preparing a place for us that we can dwell with him for all of eternity. How great is that? This going away and coming back to receive his bride is pictured in the parable of the 10 virgins. The bridegroom goes away to prepare a place while the bride waits. Jewish culture and customs portray the greatest event of all times, Jesus' return.

It's Time To Be Excited

It's time to be excited because Jesus is about to show up to pull us out of this life to be with him. It's been said that Jesus will come for his church and rapture it out of this world into his presence. It is a catching away of all Christians, real ones, not religious, fake or even churchgoers that play church for other selfish reasons.

Christ warned his followers 13 times in the New Testament to not be deceived, and to watch and be ready. He wanted us to be excited about his glorious appearing. His 2nd coming is in anticipation of the wedding feast of the Lamb.

Satan, on the other hand, does not want us to be excited. He is the master deceiver; the father of lies and wants us to believe his deception rather than the signs of the times pointing to Christ's return. He will send many lies to deceive us and to rob us of the joy of living every day in anticipation of Christ's return.

Living In Anticipation

For those who believe that the Bible is the truth and is the very Word of God, it's easy to believe in and rejoice in the prophecies that tell of the rapture of God's church. The Bible tells us of others who have been taken up into heaven in very much the same way that we will be at the time of the rapture. Elijah was taken up into heaven like a whirlwind. I Kings 2:11-12 "As they were walking along and talking together, suddenly a chariot of fire and horses of fire appeared and separated the two of them, and Elijah went up to heaven in a whirlwind. Elisha saw this and cried out, "My father! My father! The chariots and horsemen of Israel! And Elisha saw him no more."

Enoch was also taken from this life so that he would not experience death. Hebrews 11:5 "By faith Enoch was taken from this life, so that he did not experience death; he could not be found, because God had taken him away. for before he was taken, he was commended as one who pleased God. Without faith it is impossible to please God, because anyone who comes to him must believe that he exists and that he rewards those who earnestly seek him." Hebrews 11:6

So, when will the church be raptured? We know there is more evidence today that Jesus is coming for his church sooner, than at any other time in history. As these signs intensify, all of us who know Christ as our savior will be looking toward heaven and waiting, with great anticipation, the coming of our Lord.

Revelation 3:10 is one of the best supporting verses from the Bible for the rapture of the church. "Because you have kept my command to persevere, I also will keep you from the hour of trial which shall come upon the whole world to test those who dwell on the earth."

I would assume that God would not bring the same type of judgment to his children, as he will on the wicked. This scripture seems to support my premise. The assumption is that believers will be taken out of harms way. Listen to what Paul tells the Thessalonians in his second letter, chapter two verses 2-15. Listen to the text again and see for yourself.

"Now we beseech you, brethren, by the coming of our Lord Jesus

Christ, and by our gathering together unto him, That ye be not soon shaken in mind, or be troubled, neither by spirit, nor by word, nor by letter as from us, as that the day of Christ is at hand. Let no man deceive you by any means: for that day shall not come, except there come a falling away first, and that man of sin be revealed, the son of perdition; Who opposeth and exalteth himself above all that is called God, or that is worshipped; so that he as God sitteth in the temple of God, shewing himself that he is God.

Remember ye not, that, when I was yet with you, I told you these things? And now ye know what withholdeth that he might be revealed in his time. For the mystery of iniquity doth already work: only he who now letteth will let, until he be taken out of the way. And then shall that wicked be revealed, whom the Lord shall consume with the spirit of his mouth, and shall destroy with the brightness of his coming: Even him, whose coming is after the working of Satan with all power and signs and lying wonders, And with all deceivableness of unrighteousness in them that perish; because they received not the love of the truth that they might be saved.

And for this cause God shall send them strong delusion, that they should believe a lie: That they all might be damned who believed not the truth, but had pleasure in unrighteousness. But we are bound to give thanks always to God for you, brethren beloved of the Lord, because God hath from the beginning chosen you to salvation through sanctification of the Spirit and belief of the truth: Whereunto he called you by our gospel, to the obtaining of the glory of our Lord Jesus Christ. Therefore, brethren, stand fast, and hold the traditions, which ye have been taught, whether by word, or our epistle." II Thess. 2:2-15

I wanted to show the context so there is no misunderstanding. Note verse seven. I have mentioned it previously…<u>he that letteth</u> is God's Holy Spirit. He is a restraining force in the world, holding evil back from its ultimate expression. When the Spirit is taken out of the way, guess what? the Spirit is in us and Jesus said He would never leave us comfortless but will be with us until the end of the age. (John 14:18)

The moment has come. It is the end of the age and we will go with the Spirit to meet Jesus in the air as Paul says in 1 Thessalonians 4:17.

There you have it. The rapture or sudden removal of God's children is at hand. The big question now is will you be left behind? Non-believers will be left to face the great tribulation where God pours out his wrath upon the wicked. You don't want to be in that group of folks. Get your heart right with God, make Jesus your Lord and Savior, and start looking and being ready for His return.

The Bridegroom is coming. The Philadelphia church has issued its midnight cry. The foolish virgins are off looking for who knows what. The door of salvation is about to be closed. Today is the day of salvation but tomorrow will just be too late.

If you are one of the virgins that fell asleep and now are awake, don't be foolish. Repent and be Born Again. Fill yourself with God's Spirit and His Word and be ready, ever watching and praying for the Bridegroom to appear.

I believe it will occur in my lifetime. But, even if it doesn't, I will keep alert with my ear attuned to his voice and my heart filled with his Word to walk with him by faith every day. I will occupy until I see him face to face.

IN A TWINKLE OF A EYE

In the twinkle of an eye,
The Lord will come for me.
Before you can even blink,
I'll be with Jesus in eternity.

In the twinkle of an eye,
The trump of God will sound,
And all who love the Lord
Will be homeward bound.

In the twinkle of an eye,
The World will fall into despair.
When God's wrath is poured out,
Upon all who do not care.

In the twinkle of an eye,
We shall shout the victory.
Spared from His judgment,
To complete our divine destiny.

Written By
John Marinelli

CONCLUSION

Now that we know what happened in the beginning of all things, we can understand why God has the end of the world on his calendar for the near future. He destroyed the earth with a great flood to eradicate sin but it revived and now flourishes because it hides in the hearts of human beings. We are destined to see a new heaven and a new earth for the former will pass away. It is God's judgment upon the wicked. We do not know when but we do know some other facts. Here's a few incase you missed it:

1. God will destroy the earth by fire.
2. It will happen after the 7-years of tribulation that is to come upon the people of the earth.
3. Before the end of all things, Jesus will return and take his church our of harms' way.
4. There will be a great falling away from the faith.
5. Wars and rumors of wars will progress and finally culminate in a final battle between good and evil.
6. The Anti-Christ will appear and gain power to rule over the people using the mark of the beast.
7. The survivors of the tribulation will be judged and damned or blessed according to their allegiance to the Beast or Jesus.

We are to wait, pray and look for his coming. At the same time, we are to be ever mindful of the times and seasons so we are not caught off guard or deceived. The key to it all is to stay in the Word of God. Read it every day. Learn all you can and memorize the promises and faith building stories. Here's how one of the apostles said, *"Study to shew thyself approved unto God, a workman that needs not to be ashamed, rightly dividing the word of truth."* II Timothy 2:15

I said before, at the beginning of my conclusion, "Now that we know" because I am assuming that you are a, "Born Again" Christian. However, if you are not a true believer, I want to tell you how you can become, "Born Again" and enjoy the rights and privileges of the family of God as well as escaping the wrath of God to be poured out upon the earth.

How To Be, "Born Again"

The Pew Research Center Report By Stephen Mattson 05-15-2015 has revealed that Christianity within the United States is on the decline. Here are a few excerpts from his report.

Christians are freaking out and the fear mongering has begun — many seeing it as an apocalyptic sign of the moral downfall of our secular society coinciding with a theological weakening caused by "liberalism."

Everyone seems to have an explanation of the data, and among Christians, the infighting has already begun, with most denominations rationalizing their growth, decline, or stagnancy by offering the same explanation: We're theologically sound and remaining faithful to God while everyone else is getting it wrong.

In 1965 — an astounding 93 percent of the United States population identified as Christian. But again, the sixties were hardly representative of a "Christian" nation. The point is that while the percentage of Christians in America was near its highest — the moral state of our society was far from "Christian."

In many ways, today's America is more Christian than at any previous moment in its history! Slavery and segregation has been abolished, gender inequality is on the decline, the wage gap has decreased, church communities are more diverse than ever, and people's rights related to education, jobs, and opportunities are better than ever.

Evangelical churches added more than 2 million people to their ranks, up from 59.8 million in 2007 to 62.2 million in 2014. Meanwhile, mainline churches lost 5 million people. "As a result, evangelicals now constitute a clear majority (55%) of all US Protestants," noted Pew.

The United States has the <u>largest Christian population</u> in the world, with nearly 247 million Christians, although other countries have higher percentages of Christians among their populations.

The Evaluation

We have looked at Christianity as a religion. It is the only way that we can analyze it. However, the truth be known, being a Christian originally meant that you were a follower of Jesus, a disciple.

It was not a religion to the first believers but rather a relationship. A convert to Christianity went through a time of repentance, a plea for forgiveness, and an acceptance of Jesus as Lord. Today, many churches offer a membership and boldly state that you can come just as you are, with no repentant heart, no plea for forgivemess and no need to live under the Lordship of Christ.

A Biblical Reality Check

Here's what Jesus said.

1. "If any *man* come to me, and hate not his father, and mother,

and wife, and children, and brethren, and sisters, yea, and his own life also, he cannot be my disciple." Luke 14:6

The Contemporary English Version translates this verse like this, *"You cannot be my disciple, unless you love me more than you love your father and mother, your wife and children, and your brothers and sisters. You cannot come with me unless you love me more than you love your own life."* Luke 14:6

2. "And when he had called the people to him with his disciples also, he said to them, whoever will come after me, let him deny himself, and take up his cross, and follow me. For whoever will save his life shall lose it; but whoever shall lose his life for my sake and the gospel's, the same shall save it." (Mar 8:34-35)

3. "Jesus answered and said unto him, Verily, verily, I say unto thee, except a man be born again, he cannot see the kingdom of God." John 3:3

The Pew report tells us that there are a large percentage of evangelicals that do not identify themselves as, "Born Again." What happens to these folks? Is there a different place that they will go when they die? According to Jesus, to see the kingdom of God, **you must be. "Born Again**." We know from the rest of the scriptures that there is a heaven, kingdom of God, and there is a hell, a place of torment. It's either heaven or hell. Some will benefit and some will not.

Could it be that 51% of all Methodists, 55% of all Presbyterians, 63% of all Lutherans, 29% of all Adventists and 29% of all Restorationists will not see the kingdom of God?

The Pew report also says that 15 % of all Evangelicals and 21% of all nondenominational Christians do not identify themselves as, "Born Again" This report also says that 78% of all Catholics do not identify themselves as being, "Born Again".

The Question is Why Be Born Again?

We have already discussed why we should be born again in previous chapters. Jesus said, "You Must Be "Born Again" He was talking to Nicodemus, a ruler of the Jews of that day.

Jesus went on to say, "For God so loved the world that he gave his only begotten Son, that whoever believes in him should not perish but have everlasting life. For God did not send his Son into the world to condemn the world, but that the world through him might be saved." John 3:1-16 Let's just leave it as the reason you need to be "Born Again" is to have everlasting life as John 3:16 says.

Now Hear This....Sixty-five percent of all Christians say there are multiple paths to eternal life, ultimately rejecting the exclusivity of Christ teaching, according to a survey conducted by the Pew Forum on Religion and Public Life.

The Bible Tells The Truth

All of these folks that view the path to heaven as wide go against Biblical truth. Here's what the Bible says:

1. *Neither is there salvation in any other: for there is none other name under heaven given among men, whereby we must be saved.* Acts 4:12
2. *Jesus saith unto him, I am the way, the truth, and the life: no man cometh unto the Father, but by me. John 14:6*
3. *I am the door: by me if any man enter in, he shall be saved, and shall go in and out, and find pasture.* John 10:9
4. *Behold, I stand at the door, and knock: if any man hear my voice, and open the door, I will come in to him, and will sup with him, and he with me.* Revelation 3:20

Jesus said, "Enter ye in at the strait gate: for wide *is* the gate, and broad *is* the way, that leads to destruction, and many there be which go in thereat: Because strait *is* the gate, and narrow *is* the way, which leads unto life, and few there be that find it. Matthew 7:13-14

It hurts me to read about how many people that claim to be Christian are deceived and on the wrong path in life. I guess they believe that their church will save them or their good works or the fact that they are worthy in some other way.

It is hard for most folks that are not "Born Again" to understand why there is just one way to God, yet it is true. There is only one way and that is through Jesus Christ.

The Bible is our source to prove that the one-way doctrine is valid. Acts 4:12 says, *"Neither is there salvation in any other: for there is none other name under heaven given among men, whereby we must be saved."*

I know I have spoken to this question in previous chapters but again here's why it's so important. Adam sinned against God and died spiritually. *"And the Lord God commanded the man, saying, Of every tree of the garden thou may freely eat: But of the tree of the knowledge of good and evil, thou shalt not eat of it: for in the day that thou eat thereof thou shalt surely die."* Genesis 2:16-17

His creation account shows him being made of clay and God breathing into him the breath of life. He thus became alive as a living soul. "And the Lord God formed man of the dust of the ground, and breathed into his nostrils the breath of life; and man became a living soul." Genesis 2:7. When he sinned, the breath of life was taken from him and he became a dead soul. He was truly the first of a race of the walking dead.

Life is always in relationship to God. It is his breath or Spirit that makes us alive. So, death passed upon all men for all sinned. (Romans 5:12) Their nature was now sinful. We see this in all of us and in our society.

The 2nd birth experience is by the Spirit. The Breath of Life is given to each repentant heart and their souls become alive to God. They become his children by birth.

The provability that one man could fulfill all prophecies about a Messiah that God himself said would come, (Gen.3:15), and perform fantastic miracles while here on earth, and be raised from the dead, and ascend into heaven while hundreds looked on is astronomical. But Jesus did just that…fulfilled everything that was foretold about the coming Messiah. He had to be who he said he was and therefore is truly the only way to God.

Here are a few scriptures that support the only "One-Way" doctrine.

5. …there is one God, and one mediator between God and men, the man Christ Jesus; Who gave himself a ransom for all, to be testified in due time. (I Timothy 2:5-6)
6. …Believe on the Lord Jesus Christ and thou shalt be saved… (Acts 16:31)
7. That if thou shalt confess with thy mouth the Lord Jesus, and shalt believe in thine heart that God hath raised him from the dead, THOU SHALT BE SAVED. For with the heart man believeth unto righteousness; and with the mouth confession is made unto salvation. (Romans 10:9-10)

The skeptic would say, "You mean to tell me that all the religions of the world are wrong and only Christianity is the one true religion?" Remember, Christianity is not a religion. It is a relationship born out of love between man and the one true and living God. There is no one true religion. Religion, in itself, will not get us to God. It is the blood of Christ that unlocks the door and our confession of faith in Jesus that makes it all happen. (John 14:6)

Why is Jesus the only way to God? …Because God planned it that way. He set the penalty for sin, which was death. *The soul that sin-*

neth, it shall die. (Ezekiel 18:20) In fact, Jesus was the slain Lamb of God before the foundation of the world. (Ephesians 1:3-7)

Jesus himself said, as recorded in John 14:6, "I am the way, the truth, and the life: No man cometh to the Father but by me". Christianity states that the God of the Bible is the only true God and salvation is only possible by accepting Jesus Christ, his only begotten Son as Savior and Lord. II Corinthians 5:21 says, "For he hath made him to be sin for us, who knew no sin; that we might be made the righteousness of God in him."

Validation

God validated his Son as the only way in multiple ways so we could be assured that Jesus was indeed the only way to him. Here are some to consider.

8. He claimed to be the only way as in John's record 14:6 says but validation came through miracles that proved he was who he claimed to be.
9. Eyewitnesses saw Jesus' miracles and validated them as authentic. Over 500 followers saw Jesus, after his resurrection, and watched him ascend into heaven.
10. The prophets foretold of His coming, where He would be born, that he would be God in human flesh and lots more…all prophetic statements were realized in Jesus, even those like in Isaiah chapter 53 that were uttered hundreds of years before Jesus came.
11. God himself validated Jesus as his sole pathway to him. "While he was still speaking, behold, a bright cloud overshadowed them; and suddenly a voice came out of the cloud, saying, "This is my beloved Son, in whom I am well pleased. Hear ye him!"(Mathew 17:5)
12. The apostles lost their homes, wealth, and even their lives preaching the gospel. Would they do that if it were a lie? I

don't think so. They testified to the truth and were willing to die for it if necessary. (Read Foxes Book of Martyrs)
13. Thousands of believers, over several centuries have testified of how Jesus helped them and blessed them.
14. I can personally testify that I have seen the hand of the Lord in my life and communicate with him daily. I know he is the Christ.

How To Be "Born Again"

It should be obvious by now that it is essential for anyone who wants eternal life to be, "Born Again." Romans 10:9-10 will tell us how.

"That if thou shalt confess with thy mouth the Lord Jesus, and shalt believe in thine heart that God hath raised him from the dead, thou shalt be saved. For with the heart man believeth unto righteousness; and with the mouth confession is made unto salvation." Romans 10:9-10

Confessing Jesus is to acknowledge his Lordship and openly proclaim your allegiance. There is no secret society. That's why the scripture says, "With Thy Mouth."

Believing with the heart is different than with the mind. When we believe with our heart, it means to rely upon, adhere to and trust in. We are to wholly embrace the truth that God raised up Jesus from the dead after being crucified for the sins of mankind.

The power to save us and birth us into his kingdom as his child is in the fact that our heart felt belief brings us the righteousness of Christ and our open mouth of continual confession in him as our savior actually saves us.

Remember what Paul wrote to the Romans in Chapter 5. He said, in affect, that Adam was the 1st man who fell into sin and took the entire race with him. Thus death passed upon all of us. However, Jesus was the 2nd Adam or man that was sent outside of the pollution of human sinful DNA via a virgin birth to be the spotless Lamb of God and to be slain as a sacrifice for sin to abolish it forever. This is why the "New Birth" is necessary, to free us from the sin of the 1st Adam and propel us by spiritual birth into the Kingdom of God.

How Do We Know For Sure That We Are, "Born Again?"

"The Spirit itself bears witness with our spirit, that we are the children of God: And if children, then heirs; heirs of God, and jointheirs with Christ; if so be that we suffer with him, that we may be also glorified together." Romans 8:15-17

We who have believed can say that we are his children, without a doubt or any question in our minds. We can because we start out by faith but as we grow in grace the Spirit of God is continually bearing witness with our spirits. He leads us; He communicates with us, He teaches us and shows us truth and error. That's how we know for sure.

If you have never seen the hand of God in your life or heard the spirit speaking to you, you might want to go back to God and repent of your sins, ask his forgiveness and ask Jesus to come into your heart and save you. Then receive Jesus as your Lord and Savior. This is the only way you can be born again.

For by grace you have been saved through faith; and that not of yourselves, *it is* the gift of God; not as a result of works, so that no one may boast. For we are his workmanship, created in Christ Jesus for good works, which God prepared beforehand so that we would walk in them.

But now in Christ Jesus you who formerly were far off have been brought near by the blood of Christ. For he himself is our peace, who made both *groups into* one and broke down the barrier of the dividing wall, by abolishing in his flesh the enmity, *which is* the Law of commandments *contained* in ordinances, so that in himself he might make the two into one new man, *thus* establishing peace, and might reconcile them both in one body to God through the cross, by it having put to death the enmity.

So then you are no longer strangers and aliens, but you are fellow citizens with the saints, and are of God's household, having been built on the foundation of the apostles and prophets, Christ Jesus himself being the corner *stone,* in whom the whole building, being fitted together, is growing into a holy temple in the Lord, in whom you also are being built together into a dwelling of God in the Spirit. Ephesians 2:1-22 ASV

Read this again. It tells you where you were or are now and where God takes you when you are Born Again. It is truly a life changing experience.

The above scripture passage reveals 10 benefits that overtake the believer at his new birth. They are:

1. We experience God's great mercy and love…verse #4
2. We are made alive to God, given eternal life…verse #5
3. We were raised up with Christ and seated with him in Heavenly Places…. verse #6
4. We receive his Grace or unmerited favor…Verse # 8
5. We are brought close to God by the Blood of Christ…verse #13
6. Jesus becomes our peace…verse #14
7. We gain access to God through his Spirit…verse #18
8. We are no longer strangers but fellow citizens and joint heirs with Christ…verse 19

9. We are becoming a spiritual dwelling for God…verse #22
10. We are his workmanship, created in Christ Jesus unto good works that were established before we were saved so we could walk in them…v#10

We have looked at statistics that show trends and percentages of those in error. We have discussed doctrines like Jesus as the only pathway to God The Father. We have looked at benefits of being "Born Again" and why it is necessary to attain eternal life. We have seen how to be "Born Again" through repentance, a plea for forgiveness and an invitation to Jesus to enter our hearts and be Lord over our lives.

There is only one thing left to do, decide if you are, "Born Again." If not, go before the Lord and ask to be born into his kingdom. Then follow the teachings of this Jesus as written in the Bible.

The Butterfly is a great example of a sinner being transformed into a child of God.

The Story of The Butterfly

The butterfly is a beautiful example of the "Born Again" experience. It is a new creation that came out of a metamorphic change that took place in the life of a caterpillar. The body of the 1st was changed into the body of the 2nd and it is totally different that the 1st. Thus is the butterfly, never to revert back to being a caterpillar.

This new creature soars on the wings of the wind to discover a new and wonderful world full of life and beauty.

This is what happens to us. We are changing ever so slowly until one day when we will put off mortality and soar into the immortality of eternal life.

I'll leave you with this final thought. God chose to create you as a temple where he would dwell bringing heaven on earth. Your heart is rightfully his throne. You can deny him that privilege and remain the temple of Satan or you can be, "Born Again" and receive the breath of God and fulfill your divine destiny.

The beginning of the end is at hand. We need to get our houses in order, find our peace and follow after the grace of God. Watch and pray with me that we do not miss the Lord's coming. Let's not be like the foolish virgins who drifted away from the Word of God and were left behind.

May the Lord Jesus bless you with the love and grace of God.

GALLERY OF ANOINTED CHRISTIAN POEMS

I thought it might be nice to share some of my poetry with you. Sometimes a poem can say more than an entire book.

WITH EARTHEN VESSELS

Earthen vessels have never shown
such glory that once was known.
Through time and all of eternity,
came the glory of his majesty.

Full of love and full of grace,
he dwelt among the human race
to heal the sick, the blind and the lame,
to free mankind from sin and shame.

With earthen vessel he conquered all
by perfect obedience to His destined call.
For this we praise his holy name,
full of grace and full of fame.

The glory of his majesty
still shines through from eternity,
again and again to meet life's call,
in earthen vessels to conquer all.

Written By
John Marinelli

THE LIGHTHOUSE

A lighthouse is a blessing,
To the ships that toss in the sea,
For it shows them the way,
Until they can clearly see.

The rage of an angry storm
Cannot hide its brilliant light.
Nor can its awesome furry,
Rule as an endless night.

Jesus is the lighthouse,
For those who have gone astray.
The light of his love,
Offers a new and living way.

Jesus is the lighthouse,
When fear and sickness rage.
The light of his love,
Gives hope in difficult days.

So trust in the Lord,
And look for his light.
He alone is "The Lighthouse",
That guides you through the night.

Written By
John Marinelli

DON'T WORRY

Don't worry about tomorrow.
You did that yesterday.
Go on with your life,
And remember always to pray.

Ask and it shall be given to you,
But this great truth you already know.
REJOYCE AND BE HAPPY, Why?
Your harvest comes from what you grow.

I will say it again and even more,
Until it becomes crystal clear.
Tomorrow will take care of itself,
But worry is another word for fear.

Now here's what I want you to do.
Trust in the Lord and be of good cheer.
Drop the worry from your vocabulary
And cast out that demon of fear.

Written By
Rev. John Marinelli

I AM THERE

"I AM" There,
At the end of your broken dreams,
Before the sun rises over your day,
Prior to those tear-filled streams.

"I AM" There,
Down that road of despair,
When all seems to be lost,
And no one seems to care.

"I AM" There,
Over all of life's twists and turns,
When tomorrow is all but gone,
And when you are full of concerns.

"I AM" There,
Sayeth the Lord of Host,
To bring you hope and peace,
And the power of my Holy Ghost.

"I AM" There,
To be sure you make it through,
In the midst of every trial,
To bless your life and deliver you.

"I AM" There

Written By
John Marinelli

A HIGHWAY CALLED HOLINESS

He placed my feet on
a highway called "Holiness"
that led my soul
to the throne of God.

Amidst the cheers of Angels,
I walk wearing His holy gown.
Onward towards heaven's throne,
while evil cast its awful frown.

My eyes were opened
that I might see
both the good and the evil
that sought after me.

I walk the highway called Holiness
that crosses all of time,
towards the throne of God,
leaving this world behind.

Written By
John Marinelli

A WHISPER IN THE WIND

There's a whisper in the wind,
That lingers both day and night.
A champion of truth and justice,
By the power of His might.

A word in due season,
That echoes from deep within.
A voice out of nowhere,
Reproving the world of Sin.

Look there, in the street,
And here, by the shores of the sea.
There's a whisper hidden in the wind,
A voice from eternity.

There's a calling from God.
His voice is hidden in the wind.
In a whisper, He speaks to our hearts,
With the love and counsel of a friend.

Listen for the whisper,
All who seek to know.
It is God's Holy Spirit,
Telling you which way to go.

Poem By
John Marinelli

THE WAY MAKER

Only Jesus can make a way,
Through the difficulties of life.
He alone is the Lord,
Over life's sorrows and strife.

He is the "Way Maker,"
When there is no visible way.
He will make the way known,
As though it were the light of day.

He will make a way,
For those of humble heart.
He will clear away the rubble,
Restoring what Satan broke apart.

Jesus is the "Way Maker."
A friend to all who are lost.
He has made the way,
Paying sin's incredible cost.

The way to the Maker,
Is through his only Son.
He alone is the "Way Maker,"
Until life's battles are won.

Written By
John Marinelli

FRAGILE FLOWER RED

As a flower in earthen sod,
I bloom for thee, oh God.
To blossom with the turn of spring,
to be to you, a beautiful thing.

I lift my Fragile Flower Red
upward from my earthen bed,
to draw light from God above,
strength and peace and joy and love.

As a flower, I bloom for Thee,
that passersby may stop and see.
Your fragrance and beauty I am,
flowered in grace as a man.

As a flower in earthen sod,
I bloom for Thee, oh God.
Upward, I lift my head,
as a Fragile Flower Red.

Written By
John Marinelli

I FIND MYSELF IN GOD

I find myself in God.
He is my, "Everything."
I know that He is Lord,
My life, my Hope, and King.

I find myself in God,
Not the ways of sin.
Nor do I look to others,
To know who I really am.

I find myself in God,
To whom I bow on bended knee.
He alone is my joy and strength
And where I want to be.

Written By
John Marinelli

WISE MEN STILL SEEK HIM

Wise men still seek Him
Who appeared so long ago.
They come now by grace
Through faithful hearts aglow

Wise men still seek Him,
For he is their "Bread of Life"
A sustaining inner strength
Through times of sorrow or strife.

Wise men still seek Him
The Christ of Calvary
God's only begotten Son
Crucified as sin's penalty.

Wise men still seek Him,
Jesus, God in human array.
King of kings and Lord of lords,
Born to earth on Christmas Day.

Written By
John Marinelli

ABOUT THE AUTHOR

Rev. John Marinelli

Rev. Marinelli is an ordained minister, He has formed and been pastor of one church in Wisconsin and was the pastor of another in Alabama. He has also been a youth minister and evangelism director over the years.

Rev. Marinelli has authored several books including: "Original Story Poems", "The Art of Writing Christian Poetry," "Pulpit Poems," "Moonlight & Mistletoe," "The Mysterious Stranger," "With Eagles Wings," "Mysteries & Miracles," "It Came To Pass," Why Do The Righteous Suffer," and "Believer's Handbook of Battle Strategies."

John is an accomplished Christian poet. He also dabbles in song-writing and writing one act Christian plays.

He is the Vice President of Have A Heart For Companion Animals, Inc., a "No Kill" animal welfare organization...

www.haveaheart.us

Rev. Marinelli is now retired from the sales and marketing arena after spending over 40 years in business-to-business and non-profit marketing.

Rev. Marinelli enjoys writing Christian fiction stories, playing chess, singing karaoke and a retired lifestyle in sunny Florida.

For More Info or eMail Communication

Contact johnmarinelli@embarqmail.com

The End

www.ingramcontent.com/pod-product-compliance
Lightning Source LLC
Chambersburg PA
CBHW070733020526
44118CB00035B/1250